CHRONOLOGY AND DOCUMENTARY HANDBOOK OF THE STATE OF
ARIZONA

ELLEN LLOYD TROVER,
State Editor

WILLIAM F. SWINDLER,
Series Editor

1972 OCEANA PUBLICATIONS, INC./Dobbs Ferry, New York

This is Volume 3 in the series CHRONOLOGIES AND DOCUMENTARY HANDBOOKS OF THE STATES.

© Copyright 1972 by Oceana Publications, Inc.

Library of Congress Cataloging in Publication Data
Main entry under title:

Chronology and documentary handbook of the State of Arizona.

(Chronologies and documentary handbooks of the States, v. 3)
   SUMMARY: Contains a chronology of historical events from 1526 to 1970, a directory of political figures, an outline of the state constitution, and copies of five historical documents.
   Bibliography: p.
   1. Arizona--History--Chronology. 2. Arizona--History--Sources. [1. Arizona--History] I. Trover, Ellen Lloyd, ed. II. Series
F811.C53   979.1   72-5199
ISBN 0-379-16128-1

Manufactured in the United States of America

CONTENTS

INTRODUCTION v

CHRONOLOGY (1526-1970) 1

BIOGRAPHICAL DIRECTORY 35

OUTLINE OF CONSTITUTION 39

SELECTED DOCUMENTS 55

    Adventures in Apache Country 55

    An Arizona Episode (Pearl Hart) 83

    The Last of the Territories 89

    Veto on Arizona Statehood 105

    Arizona and the Recall of the Judiciary . 115

SELECTED BIBLIOGRAPHY 119

NAME INDEX 121

INTRODUCTION

This projected series of *Chronologies and Documentary Handbooks of the States* will ultimately comprise fifty separate volumes – one for each of the states of the Union. Each volume is intended to provide a concise ready reference of basic data on the state, and to serve as a starting point for more extended study as the individual user may require. Hopefully, it will be a guidebook for a better informed citizenry – students, civic and service organizations, professional and business personnel, and others.

The editorial plan for the *Handbook* series falls into five divisions: (1) a chronology of selected events in the history of the state; (2) a short biographical directory of the principal public officials, e.g., governors, Senators and Representatives; (3) an analytical outline of the state constitution; (4) the text of some representative documents illustrating main currents in the political, economic, social or cultural history of the state; and (5) a selected bibliography for those seeking further or more detailed information. Most of the data found in the present volume, in fact, have been taken from one or another of these references.

The user of these *Handbooks* may ask why the full text of the state constitution, or the text of constitutional documents which affected the history of the state, have not been included. There are several reasons: In the case of the current constitution, the text in almost all cases is readily available from one or more official agencies within the state. In addition, the current constitutions of all fifty states, as well as the federal Constitution, are regularly kept up to date in the definitive collection maintained by the Legislative Drafting Research Fund of Columbia University and published by the publisher of the present series of *Handbooks*. These texts are available in most major libraries under the title, *Constitutions of the United States: National and State*, in two volumes, with a companion volume, the *Index Digest of State Constitutions*.

Finally, the complete collection of documents illustrative of the constitutional development of each state, from colonial or territorial status up to the current constitution as found in the Columbia University collection, is being prepared for publication in a multi-volume series by the present series editor. Whereas the present series of *Handbooks* is intended for a wide range of interested citizens, the series of annotated constitutional materials in the volumes of *Sources and Documents of U.S. Constitutions* is primarily for the specialist in government, history or law. This is not to suggest that the general citizenry may not profit equally from referring to these materials; rather, it points up the separate purpose of the *Handbooks*, which is to guide the user to these and other sources of authoritative information with which he may systematically enrich his knowledge of this state and its place in the American Union.

William F. Swindler
Series Editor

CHRONOLOGY

1526 — Don Jose de Basconales reportedly crossed portion of Arizona on exploration trip from Mexico to Zuni territory.

1539 — Friar Marcos de Niza, one of first to seek for fabled "Seven Cities of Cibola," reported viewing various native "stone cities" (pueblos) and claimed all of territory for New Spain.

1540 — Francisco Vasquez de Coronado led major expedition in search of "Seven Cities of Cibola," entering parts of present day New Mexico, Arizona and Colorado. Related expeditions led to discovery of Hopi country by Pedro de Tovar, and Grand Canyon by Garcia Lopez de Cardenas.

1582 — Antonio de Espejo led expedition which discovered silver deposits west of present-day Prescott.

1599 — Juan de Onate led an expedition east to west through Arizona area, in search of "South Sea." His subsequent expeditions extended Spanish claims as far as eastern Kansas and to mouth of Colorado River into Gulf of California.

1600 — Franciscan missionaries arrived in Hopi area and established small missions. For most of seventeenth century, mission development was sporadic while main Spanish settlement effort was concentrated in Texas.

1680 — Widespread uprising among Pueblo Indians wiped out many missions and massacred inhabitants.

1692 — Spurred by the need to establish a stronger regime in this area, Mexico authorized Father Eusebio Kino to construct new missions with closer and more frequent contacts with established centers in New Spain. San Gabriel de Guevavi Mission, and related missions in Santa Cruz and San Pedro valleys, were established.

1696	San Jose de Tumacacori Mission founded.
1700	Major link in Father Kino's administrative program was Mission San Xavier del Bac, near Tucson. In the course of his mission building, within a concentrated area from Nogales and Tucson to the mouth of the Colorado River, Father Kino completed elaborate maps of the region and consolidated its communications with Mexico.
1752	For another half-century, Spanish authorities preferred to develop silver resources of interior of Central America and protect shipping routes along West Coast and Gulf Coast rather than push further into Arizona. In this year, however, enough settlers migrated into Santa Cruz valley to warrant establishment of a *presidio* (military post) at Tubac.
1767	Jesuits were expelled from New Spain. The following year the Franciscans under Father Francisco Tomas Garces took over the Arizona missions.
1772	*Reglamento* of Spanish authorities directed *presidio* at Tubac to be moved to Tucson. This was accomplished in 1776. Meantime, Father Garces began continuing series of missionary expeditions into northern Arizona, seeking to convert warlike tribes and prepare for extension of mission system.
1781	Father Garces and his combined military-missionary force were massacred by Yuma Indians.
1782	Punitive expedition under General Teodoro de Croix ravaged Yuma villages.
1824	Mexico, which had won its independence two years earlier, created Territory of Nuevo Mexico which included Arizona. First American trappers appeared on Gila, Salt and Colorado rivers.

CHRONOLOGY

1838   Tubac became a *pueblo*, or civil governmental unit, instead of military post. This was symptom of long-delayed establishment of settled society in the area.

1846   *May 13.* United States declared war on Mexico. Colonel Stephen W. Kearny, commanding the Army of the West, captured Santa Fe in New Mexico and marched across Arizona en route to California.

December 17. Lt. Col. Philip St. George Cooke's "Mormon Battalion" drove out Mexican garrison and took possession of Tucson in name of United States.

1848   *February 2.* Mexican War ended by treaty of Guadaloupe-Hidalgo, with cession of most of land north of Gila River and provision for eventual survey to settle on boundary.

Unsettled conditions after war led to Apache uprising and destruction of Tubac and Tumacacori. Survivors moved to Tucson.

1849   United States executed treaty with Navajo tribe to settle on their territorial limits in newly acquired territory.

First American military post established at Fort Defiance.

October 12. Emigrant party under Charles E. Pancoast completed trip down Gila River, marked by birth of first Anglo-Saxon child in this territory. He was named "Gila."

1850   *April 23.* First commercial ferry at Yuma Crossing, established earlier in this year, was scene of Yuma Indian attack and massacre.

September 9. Congress organized a Territory of New Mexico, including Arizona, in an "omnibus bill."

1850 — Admission of California and organization of Utah Territory in same bill, followed by Kansas-Nebraska Act in 1854, completed territorial organization of continental United States.

First territorial census of both New Mexico-Arizona area reported population of 61,547.

1852 — First government exploration of northern Arizona was carried out by Captain Lorenzo Sitgreaves.

Schooner *Capacity* arrived via Gulf of California at mouth of Colorado river and unloaded materials for construction of a steamboat. Later the first steamboat, the *Uncle Sam*, reached Yuma.

1853 — *December 30.* Treaty modifying Mexican cession of 1848 added 45,535 acres south of Gila River to New Mexico Territory. James Gadsden, American ambassador to Mexico, had promoted the purchase as most desirable site for southern transcontinental railroad.

1854 — Copper mining in territory organized under Arizona Copper Co., a corporation formed in San Francisco.

1855 — *January 31.* Official boundary survey begun with erection of first marker at point on Rio Grande fixed by Gadsden Purchase.

1856 — *March 10.* Four companies of army dragoons quartered in Tucson, to protect mining, stagecoach and other interests from Indian raids. Meantime, military authorities were planning to introduce camels as possible transport auxiliaries in desert area.

August 26. Territorial residents convened in Tucson to petition Congress for division of the territory in anticipation of early qualification for statehood. A delegate to Congress, Nathan B. Cook, was elected

1856   but never seated. Residents complained that Congress was neglecting the needs of the rapidly developing western portion of the New Mexico Territory.

1857   *March 1.* Reflecting the confident and imperialistic spirit of the period, a band of "filibusters" under Henry A. Crabb invaded the Mexican state of Sonora in hope of seizing it. The adventurers were ambushed and wiped out by Mexican militia.

June 22. A government contract was let for semi-monthly mail delivery by stagecoach between San Antonio and San Diego by way of Tucson. Because passengers frequently had to ride muleback from Yuma to the coast, the line became known as the "Jackass Mail."

December 8. President James Buchanan recommended creating separate Territory of Arizona. Anticipating that Congress would act favorably on the proposal, civic meeting at Tucson sent Lieutenant Sylvester Mowry to Washington as its delegate. Since Congress failed to act, he was not seated.

1858   *September 3.* Civic group again petitioned Congress for separate territorial status and reelected Mowry as their delegate, but again Congress failed to act.

1859   *March 3.* First territorial newspaper, the *Weekly Arizonian*, begun in Tubac.

July 3. Residents of Tucson and Mesilla repeated the annual tactic of electing a delegate to Congress to dramatize their campaign for territorial recognition. Congress again ignored the matter.

1860   *April 2.* Continuing the campaign for territorial status, Tucson convention drew up a territorial constitution in order to create a provisional government until Congress acted. Meantime, the territorial legislature in New Mexico had created the

1860 — first county in the western half of the territory, naming it Arizona County.

Census figures taken for first time in western part of New Mexico Territory listed 6,482 persons in this area. To government officials in Washington, this was sufficient justification for refusal to act on petitions for separate territorial status.

1861 — *February 4*. Cochise, leader of Apaches, met with army officers under Lieutenant George H. Bascom for peace talks. Bascom's treacherous attempt to capture Cochise provoked a decade of savage Apache depredations in area.

March 16. Secession convention met in Mesilla and repudiated the "Black Republican Administration" of Abraham Lincoln. It declared Arizona to be attached to the Confederate States of America. The action was partly in resentment of what many persons felt was Congressional disinterest in the region and partly a reflection of Southern economic interest, stemming from persistent plans for transcontinental railroad from south Atlantic coast to Pacific.

August 1. Lt. Col. John R. Baylor of the Confederate army took possession of Mesilla and declared Arizona to be a territory. In hope of official recognition, Tucson meeting sent Granville Oury to Confederate Congress as representative, but he was not seated.

1862 — *January 18*. Confederate Congress passed statute creating Arizona Territory.

February 28. Capt. Sherod Hunter of Confederate Texan forces entered Tucson and took possession of territory.

March 11. Marcus H. McWillie was formally seated in Confederate Congress as territorial delegate.

CHRONOLOGY

1862   *March 12.* Belatedly awakening to depth of territorial feeling, U.S. Congress received a bill from Congressman James H. Ashley of Ohio, creating a federal Territory of Arizona.

April 15. "Farthest west battle" of Civil War, a skirmish with units of California Column near Yuma, led to Confederate evacuation of Tucson. California Column entered Tucson the next month.

1863   *February 20.* Arizona Territorial Bill passed by Congress, and was signed into law February 24. President Lincoln appointed as first territorial governor John A. Gurley, who died before formal organization of government.

December 29. Territorial government formally launched at Navajo Springs, designated by Congress as temporary capital. As governor to succeed Gurley, John N. Goodwin had been appointed.

1864   *January 6.* Col. Kit Carson led attack on Navajos in Canyon de Chelly, breaking power of tribe and compelling surrender of 12,000 members in following months.

April 9. Governor Goodwin proclaimed establishment of civil law in territory and creation of three judicial districts, at Tucson, La Paz and Prescott.

May 30. Territorial government, which had been seated first at Fort Whipple, was moved to Granite Creek, renamed Prescott.

July 18. Charles D. Poston, mining operator and territorial leader, was named first delegate to Congress. A native of Kentucky, Poston had come to California during the gold rush and subsequently settled in Arizona.

1864 — *September 26.* Legislature created first four counties: Mohave, Pima, Yavapai and Yuma. It enacted legislation establishing a university and adopted a civil code known as the Howell Code.

December 26. Territorial supreme court held its first session in Prescott.

1865 — *March 4.* Governor Goodwin succeeded Poston as delegate to Congress. A native of Maine, Goodwin had recently served one term as Congressman from that state, before being appointed territorial governor. After this term in Congress he did not return to Arizona but took up law practice in New York.

As third governor of the territory another ex-Congressman, Robert C. McCormick of New York, was appointed. McCormick, a war correspondent during the Civil War, established both *Arizona Miner* at Prescott and *Arizona Citizen* at Tucson. He served as acting governor and then as governor before also being elected to delegate's seat.

1867 — *May 4.* Coles Bashford, first attorney general of territory, was seated as territorial delegate. A lawyer in New York and later Wisconsin, he had become the first Republican governor of that state in 1855; after this term he moved to Arizona and was active in law and business in territory, both before and after his single term in Congress.

May 5. Pah-Ute County, created by legislature from part of Mohave county, was divided between section of territory transferred to Nevada by Congress. Remainder was merged again into Mohave county.

September 4. Legislature transferred capital from Prescott to Tucson. Records and offices relocated by November 1.

CHRONOLOGY

1868   *June 1.* First of series of government treaties with Navajos created Indian reservation and provided for education and other services for ten year period in return for cession of lands outside reservation.

1869   *April 7.* Anson P. K. Safford became territorial governor.

May 4. Richard C. McCormick elected delegate to Congress, to first of three terms.

Congress changed sessions of legislature from annual to biennial.

1870   *October 20.* Townsite for present city of Phoenix laid out.

Decennial census reported territorial population of 9,658.

1871   *January 11.* Maricopa county created out of part of Yavapai. Legislature enacted general public school statute.

June. General George Crook assumed command of military department of Arizona, with instructions to reduce the continuing harrassment of towns by Indian tribes. His other assignment was the attempted reduction in stagecoach holdups by highwaymen.

1872   *July 30.* San Francisco corporation formed to develop alleged diamond fields in northern Arizona. Based partly on rumor and partly on confidence game, the project became known as the "Great Diamond Hoax."

October 12. Army pacification program succeeded in negotiating peace treaty with Cochise, chief of Chiricahua Apaches.

1873 *August 6.* Vigilante group, the Law and Order Society, lynched four convicted murderers on one of public streets in Tucson.

1875 *January 6.* Pinal county created from parts of Yavapai, Maricopa and Pima. Legislature offered bounties for discovery of artesian water.

October 2. Typical stagecoach holdup occurred between Phoenix and Florence, with robbery of $1,400.

December 6. Hiram S. Stephens of Tucson defeated McCormick for delegate seat. An Army veteran and territorial legislator, he served two terms.

1876 *January 30.* Severe smallpox epidemic virtually isolated La Paz.

July 4. Party of immigrants from Boston celebrated Fourth near San Francisco Mountains and name the site Flagstaff.

1877 *January 11.* Legislature moved capital back to Prescott.

March 3. In effort to establish series of strong points to protect border area and stagecoach routes, Camp (later Fort) Huachuca was established near Tucson.

April 5. John P. Hoyt became governor. He had been appointed territorial secretary the previous year, and had undertaken a general revision of the territorial laws which was adopted by the legislature and known as the Hoyt Code.

1878 *June 8.* John C. Fremont, veteran explorer and frontier leader known as "The Pathfinder," was appointed territorial governor.

CHRONOLOGY

1879
January 6. Apache County created out of part of Yavapai. Legislature passed bill for a state lottery but Post Office refused to permit use of mails to carry it out.

March 18. John G. Campbell of Prescott was seated as territorial delegate. Born in Scotland and raised in New York, he had been a California "49-er" before moving to Arizona and setting up in general mercantile business.

1880
May 1. First issue of widely-read territorial newspaper, the Tombstone *Epitaph*, published in a tent.

October 3. President Rutherford B. Hayes on nationwide tour made stop at Maricopa to confer with Indian leaders.

October 4. John N. Irwin appointed governor of territory.

Census showed great jump in population to 40,440 persons.

1881
January 3. Cochise, Graham and Yuma counties created out of parts of Maricopa, Pima and Yavapai.

July 1. Atlantic and Pacific Railroad, part of a transcontinental network, entered Arizona.

September 16. Ineffectiveness of military authorities in curbing Indian depredations led to mass meeting in Phoenix with demands for stronger government action against Apaches.

October 26. Gunfight at the O. K. Corral in Tombstone between Earp, Clanton and McLowry gangs resulted in three deaths in 30 seconds.

1881 — *December 5.* Granville H. Oury of Florence was seated as Arizona delegate in Congress. Virginia-born and Missouri educated, he had been a California "49-er" before moving to territory where he practiced law and served as territorial judge and later attorney general. He had been territorial delegate to Confederate Congress.

1882 — *February 6.* Frederick A. Tritle appointed territorial governor.

July 23. Mormon settlers purchased 80 acres of land west of Phoenix to found the town of Tempe.

1883 — *August 12.* Stagecoach holdups continued to plague military and territorial authorities. On this night, two stage lines were held up on different runs, and a Wells Fargo messenger was killed.

1885 — *March 12.* Governor Tritle signed legislation creating the University of Arizona.

April 11. Mass meeting held in Florence to organize campaign against James Addison Reavis and his claim to "barony of Arizona," a claim based on fraudulent Spanish land grants and including towns of Casa Grande, Clifton, Florence, Globe, Mesa, Phoenix, Solomville and Tempe.

October 18. C. Meyer Zulick appointed governor of territory, the first Democratic appointee.

November 15. First through passenger train, from San Diego to Mississippi Valley, began its run through Arizona.

December 7. New territorial delegate seated. He was Curtis C. Bean, born in New Hampshire, later a practicing lawyer in Tennessee, who had lived in Arizona since 1868 engaging in business and mining.

CHRONOLOGY

1886   *March 29.* General Crook presumably ended long campaign against Apaches by effecting surrender of Geronimo and his leading warriors, but the famed Indian chief and 20 of his best men escaped.

August 25. Lieutenant Charles B. Gatewood, with two friendly Indians, sought out Geronimo and persuaded him to surrender once more, to General Nelson A. Miles.

1887   *December 7.* New territorial delegate, Marcus A. Smith of Tombstone, took seat in Congress. He was a Kentucky-born attorney and early Democratic political leader in territory.

1889   *April 9.* Lewis Wolfley became governor. He quickly incurred unpopularity, first by vetoing a bill creating Coconino County, then by refusing to call for election of delegates to a constitutional convention.

1890   *January 28.* Epidemic of spotted fever swept Gila River settlements.

February 22. Walnut Grove dam collapsed, causing widespread death and property damage along Hassayampa River.

October 4. Governor Wolfley replaced by John N. Irwin.

Decennial census showed population of 88,243.

1891   *January 19.* Coconino County created out of Yavapai County.

February 18. Widespread floods on Gila, Salt and Colorado rivers damaged numerous territorial settlements and washed out railroad beds.

April 21. President Benjamin Harrison on special trip through West visited territory.

1891   *June 2.* In renewed drive for statehood, another constitutional convention was called in territory, eventually drawing up a draft constitution and petitioning Congress for admission. There was no response from Congress.

June 7. Yuma began diverting water from Colorado river for irrigation purposes, one of many projects by communities and individuals which precipitated legal battles over rights to scarce water.

October 1. University of Arizona opened for classes.

1892   *May 11.* Nathan O. Murphy, who had been serving as acting governor, formally appointed as tenth governor of territory. Murphy brothers had been in territory for ten years, establishing successful business empire.

May 19. Stagecoach service begun between Flagstaff and the Grand Canyon.

May 25. Arizona Medical Association established in Phoenix.

June 22. Casa Grande ruins declared a national reservation by President Harrison.

1893   *April 5.* Louis C. Hughes appointed territorial governor by President Grover Cleveland. A veteran newspaperman and maverick Democratic politican, Hughes fought running battle with state and national party leaders throughout his administration.

1894   *March 30.* Special court hearing private land claims voided large number of Spanish grants along border, thus ending a long series of disputes which had clouded titles to large tracts.

1895   *January 21.* Navajo County created from western half of Apache County.

CHRONOLOGY

1895 — *December 2.* Ex-governor Murphy took seat as territorial delegate to Congress.

1896 — *March 30.* Governor Hughes was removed from office as climax to continuing battle with state and national party leaders and alleged subversion of Congressional policy on public lands. President Grover Cleveland appointed Benjamin Franklin, a descendant of famed historical figure, as governor.

August 12. Yaqui Indian uprising brought troops from Fort Huachuca and armed posses of citizens to meet danger.

1897 — *March 15.* Marcus Smith, longtime Democratic power in territory, resumed seat in Congress he had first held in 1887.

May 19. Myron H. McCord, former Wisconsin Congressman and protege of President William McKinley, was appointed territorial governor.

July 18. McCord's appointment was confirmed after spirited opposition to him in Congress and in territory.

1898 — *July 19.* McCord resigned as governor in order to lead territorial regiment to Cuba in Spanish-American War. Former Governor Murphy appointed to fill vacancy.

1899 — *January 16.* Santa Cruz County created out of part of Pima County.

December 4. John F. Wilson, state attorney general and leader of state Democratic faction which had fought both Hughes and McCord, seated as delegate in Congress.

1900 — *May 8.* President McKinley, on special train tour of West, paid visits to Tucson and Phoenix but

1900   disappointed many residents by making no mention of statehood.

Census report for territory showed 122,931 persons.

1901   *January 21.* Legislature convened for first time in new state house in Phoenix. Governor Murphy was authorized to create corps of Arizona Rangers, intended like Texas Rangers to provide special force to establish law and order in area.

March 18. Saguaro cactus blossom adopted as state flower.

October 26. Mass meeting in Phoenix on statehood question resulted in appointment of special delegation to lay case before Congress.

December 2. "Mark" Smith again seated as territorial delegate.

1902   *May 7.* President Theodore Roosevelt during tour of territory -- in which he evaded statehood question -- received Murphy's resignation as governor following months of criticism of Murphy in Congress.

July 1. Alexander O. Brodie, protege of Theodore Roosevelt, appointed territorial governor.

1903   *January 22.* Spectacular head-on crash of Southern Pacific trains near Vail's Station caused 22 deaths and large number of injuries.

February 5. Legislature wired protest to Congress over bill proposing to admit Arizona and New Mexico as single state.

October 5. First major irrigation project of federal government, Tonto Basin (Roosevelt) Dam, authorized by Department of Interior.

CHRONOLOGY

1903   *November 9.* John F. Wilson replaced Marcus Smith as territorial delegate.

December 28. Fire damaged state capitol.

1905   *February 10.* President Roosevelt appointed Joseph M. Kibbey as territorial governor. As member of territorial supreme court, Kibbey had written renowned decision in 1892 affirming priority in water rights to first beneficial user of water from a stream.

May 28. Bipartisan league against joint statehood formed to oppose bill to admit Arizona and New Mexico as single state.

July 12. Special Congressional committee arrived in Arizona to study claims of territory for separate statehood.

December 4. Marcus Smith again won seat in Congress as delegate.

December 5. President Roosevelt in annual message to Congress recommended admission of New Mexico and Arizona as single state. Mass meetings throughout territory voiced protests.

1906   *March 9.* Senate rejected House bill proposing joint statehood, substituting proposal of Senator Joseph Foraker of Ohio that residents of territory be asked to vote on question.

November 6. Referendum on joint statehood proposal rejected proposal by 16,265 to 3,141.

December 8. Petrified Forest National Monument created.

1907   *August 30.* President Roosevelt acceded to demands for separate statehood and announced administration support for new bill.

1908 — *January 11.* First Grand Canyon National Monument created.

1909 — *February 17.* Geronimo, famous Apache chief, died in captivity.

May 6. Richard E. Sloan, member of territorial supreme court, appointed as last territorial governor.

October 13. President William Howard Taft on special tour of West delivered speeches at Phoenix, Tempe and Yuma, promising administration support for statehood.

December 15. Ralph H. Cameron of Flagstaff replaces Mark Smith as last territorial delegate.

1910 — *June 20.* Congress finally passed enabling act for Arizona statehood.

September 12. Delegates to state constitutional convention elected, with Democrats having 36 to 16 advantage.

October 10. Constitutional convention opened in Phoenix. Strongly progressive document, including initiative, referendum and recall adopted in spite of warnings that President opposed provision for recall of judges.

Census figures showed 204,354 persons in territory on eve of statehood.

1911 — *February 9.* Constitution with recall provision adopted by voters of territory, 12,187 to 3,302.

April 15. President Taft announced he intended to veto statehood bill because of provision for recall of judges, which he questioned as threat to judicial independence.

CHRONOLOGY

1911   *June 2.* Henry F. Ashurst and M.G. Burns, political opponents for first seat in U.S. Senate, engaged in fist fight in Prescott.

August 8. Statehood bill passed by Congress.

August 14. President Taft vetoed Arizona statehood bill and returned it to Congress with firm statement of his opposition to judicial recall.

August 19. Congress adopted new statehood bill without recall provision.

August 21. President Taft signed amended statehood bill.

December 12. First state elections held. George W.P. Hunt, president of constitutional convention, elected first state governor. U.S. Senators: Henry F. Ashurst and Marcus A. Smith; U.S. Representative: Carl Hayden.

1912   *November 5.* State constitutional amendment restoring judicial recall approved by voters.

1913   *April 3.* An act providing for police courts in incorporated cities and towns became law.

April 12. Governor Hunt vetoed penal code adopted by the legislature because it limited pardoning powers.

April 25. The legislature passed a three-cent-a-mile railroad fare law.

May 17. The legislature passed a new penal code providing for capital punishment. Gov. Hunt vetoed it but his veto was overridden.

1913

June 5. Secretary of State ruled there were sufficient signatures obtained to initiate an anti-capital punishment law.

August 19. A law establishing an eight-hour work day for women went into effect.

December 8. Gov. Hunt filed protest with Gen. Venustiano Carranza of Mexico over the executions of prisoners of war by Pancho Villa. Carranza replied they were necessary and humane.

December 13. Yuma asked Gov. Hunt for troops to protect the border against Mexican marauders.

1914

February 19. The Arizona Supreme Court voided the three-cent fare law passed by the legislature. Held: the state has no right to set rates for public service corporation.

April 21. The U.S. took Vera Cruz; Governor Hunt asked permission to call out the Arizona National Guard.

April 23. As the U.S. and Mexico moved toward war the Arizona National Guard at Yuma was called out to patrol the Colorado River border.

April 28. Governor Hunt withdrew state guard from Yuma when the War Department failed to send regulars. Yuma citizens formed a home guard.

August 13. Federal Court in San Francisco ruled that Arizona State Corporation Commission had authority to regulate rates of public utilities.

August 14. President Wilson signed reclamation measure giving farmers 10 years of grace in repaying government loans used for construction of dams and canals.

CHRONOLOGY

1914
November 4. Governor Hunt re-elected. The State also voted for prohibition, the three-cent law and an 80% law compelling employers to give preference to electors or native-born citizens.

December 11. General Tasker H. Bliss was shot at as he inspected the American defenses at Naco. Washington warned the Mexicans that the U.S. would reply with artillery if firing continued into U.S. territory.

1915
January 7. Federal court declared unconstitutional the new Arizona law making it illegal for employers to use more than 20 per cent alien labor on their pay rolls.

September 20. The Supreme Court upheld the 8-hour work law for women.

November 2. The U.S. Supreme Court declared the alien labor law void.

November 26. U.S. forces at Nogales, Arizona under Colonel W. H. Sage and Mexican forces under Obregon, who were seeking to drive Villa out of Nogales, Sonora, engaged in a 30 minute small-arms battle across the border. Later both commanders met and apologized.

1916
February 13. The Arizona Supreme Court ruled that liquor could be brought into the state for personal use.

March 21. Governor Hunt ordered the Arizona National Guard up to war strength as a result of the threat after Villa's raid on Columbus, New Mexico.

May 10. The U.S. Government ordered the Arizona National Guard to the Mexican border.

1916

July 6. The voters rejected, 21,255 to 18,061, an amendment to the constitution which was a workmens' compensation law favored by mine owners.

November 7. Thomas E. Campbell, Republican, was declared to have defeated Hunt for governor by 30 votes.

December 16. Governor Hunt's effort to contest the election of Thomas E. Campbell was denied by the Superior Court in Phoenix.

1917

January 3. Hunt refused to vacate the governor's office and Campbell opened a temporary office at his home. The state treasurer and state auditor said they would not honor checks signed by Campbell.

January 27. The Supreme Court declared Thomas E. Campbell to be Governor de facto, of Arizona.

March 15. Overruling the national reclamation commission, Franklin K. Lane, Secretary of the Interior, ruled that the Salt River Valley reclamation project was completed, that the Roosevelt Dam was part of the project and that the federal government should turn the completed job over to the Water Users Association.

May 22. Superior Court Judge R.C. Stanford ruled that examination of the ballots showed Campbell defeated Hunt for governor by 30 to 50 votes.

October 5. A presidential commission arrived in the state to study the labor strikes.

December 22. The Supreme Court reversed the trial court verdict and declared G.W.P. Hunt legally elected governor.

1918   *May 24.* The Legislature passed a resolution ratifying the proposed prohibition amendment to the Constitution of the United States.

May 28. Matthew Rivers, a Pima Indian, was killed at Catigny, France. He was the first Arizonan to die in World War I.

February 1. By a joint memorial, the Legislature urged Congress to buy the State of Lower California, the Coronado Islands and 10,000 square miles in the State of Sonora from Mexico.

November 5. Thomas E. Campbell was elected governor.

1919   *January 21.* By joint resolution, the State Legislature requested Congress to pass the National Woman Suffrage Amendment.

March 25. Governor Campbell vetoed a bill providing for reading of the Bible in public schools.

March 26. The Legislature appropriated $100,000 to co-operate with U.S. Department of Interior on surveys and preliminary studies for construction of storage or diversion dams to increase the productivity of the land.

August 16. Governor Campbell urged a conference of western governors to adopt a plan for jailing profiteers, seizing their foodstuffs, and then worrying about convictions.

The legislature passed a bill modifying the Employers' Liability Act of 1912, to limit attorneys' fees in injury cases.

1920   *February 11.* The last of the military guards on the international border at Nogales were withdrawn.

1920

February 12. The State Legislature held a one-day special session and voted to ratify the 19th amendment to the U.S. Constitution which established women's suffrage.

November 2. After a bitter campaign, Campbell was re-elected governor. On May 10, it had been revealed that Mulford Winsor, former Secretary to Governor Hunt, was conducting a mail campaign for the Democratic nomination on the official letterhead of the State.

1921

February 6. Governor Campbell in conference with Mexican consuls and Arizona cotton growers learned that 8,000 Mexican cotton pickers are destitute and 2,000 in dire need. An agreement was reached to deport between 2,000 and 3,000 indigent.

February 8. Frank O. Lowden, former Governor of Illinois, addressed the fifth Arizona Legislature and urged adoption of Governor Campbell's plans for reorganization of the State government.

February 26. Governor Campbell signed an anti-alien land bill to exclude Japanese from owning farms.

March 5. The Legislature gave the governor authority to appoint a commissioner to meet representatives of California, Colorado, Nevada, New Mexico, Utah and Wyoming and to join in the formation of a Colorado River Commission. The Commission was to frame a compact for division of Colorado River waters.

March 17. Governor Campbell signed a new Workmens' Compensation Law that provided for employees automatically electing compensation under it unless they rejected it before injuries were sustained.

April 10. The U.S. Reclamation Service announced it would erect the highest dam in the world - 500 to

1921   600 feet - in Boulder Canyon, joining Nevada and Arizona.

April 11. Ralph H. Cameron succeeded Senator Smith.

July 19. The Supreme Court of Arizona held the new Workmens' Compensation Law to be in conflict with Article XVIII, Sec. 8 of the State Constitution and therefore invalid. *The Industrial Commission of Arizona v. Crisman.*

August 6. Congress passed a bill giving the seven western states right to negotiate for use of Colorado River water.

December 17. The organization of the Colorado River Commission was completed with Herbert Hoover being appointed to represent the United States.

1922   *November 7.* George W.P. Hunt defeated Campbell for governorship.

1924   *September 4.* The first Arizona Indian cast his ballot under a provision of the act of Congress granting citizenship to Indians.

November 6. G.W.P. Hunt was re-elected to his fifth term as governor in a close contest with Dwight B. Heard.

1925   *September 29.* The voters accepted, 11,879 to 9,070, an amendment to the constitution allowing for a new Workmens' Compensation Act which allowed employees to elect to be covered by the Employers Liability Act of 1912. The new law went into effect November 3, 1925, creating the Industrial Commission of Arizona.

1926   *February 11.* Governor Hunt notified the U.S. Senate that if the Boulder Dam project on the Colorado was

1926   passed, Arizona would forcibly resist building of the dam.

March 5. Senator Ralph Cameron of Arizona introduced a bill in Congress proposing construction of an irrigating and power development at Glen Canyon rather than Boulder Dam.

June 3. The State Supreme Court ruled that judges could not change or shorten a sentence once a defendant had been convicted and sentenced.

November 2. Governor Hunt defeated Edward S. Clark for governor by 399 votes. Clark had campaigned on a promise to discharge Cloyd H. Martin, president of the University of Arizona.

1927   *March 15.* The Senate bill legalizing voting machines became law.

July 19. All Arizona warehouses for rent for storage of cotton or wool became public service corporations and subject to licensing by the Arizona Corporation Commission.

July 23. Unhappy over division of tax receipts, Willcox Citizens held a mass meeting and voted unanimously for separation from Cochise County.

August 23. The California and Arizona Colorado River Commissions in conference agreed Arizona had full right to its own tributary streams.

November 28. Tucson became the terminal of the first daily passenger air service from Los Angeles to Southern Arizona.

December 5. Carl Hayden succeeded Senator Cameron. New Representative: Lewis F. Douglas, Phoenix.

1928

November 1. The Pima County Bar asked Governor Hunt to call a special session of the Legislature and rewrite the state's civil and penal code.

November 3. The Arizona Supreme Court denied the right to vote to Indians living on reservations because as "wards of the U.S." they are "persons under guardianship" and specifically disqualified for voting under the state constitution.

November 6. John C. Phillips defeated G.W.P. Hunt for governor.

December 11. The U.S. Senate voted to accept the compromise in Boulder Dam Bill giving California 200,000 acre feet less water than it wanted and depriving Arizona of 200,000 feet it said it must have. Arizona won exception of the Gila River from a provision preventing the Federal Power Commission from leasing water rights on the Colorado and its tributaries until Swing-Johnson bill became effective.

December 15. The U.S. Senate passed the Boulder Dam Bill with appropriation for $165,000,000. California received 4,400,000 acre feet, Arizona 2,800,000, Nevada 300,000.

1929

March 26. Without the sanction of any law, armed Mexican troops were transported from San Luis across American soil to reinforce the Mexican garrison at Naco.

April 4. Governor Phillips protested to Washington over the proposal of allowing Mexican federal troops to march across Arizona to Naco. He felt it would be a violation of the state Constitution.

June 25. President Hoover signed the Colorado River Compact which Arizona alone opposed out of seven western states.

1930   *March 4.* Calvin Coolidge dedicated Coolidge Dam, world's highest multiple-dome dam.

March 13. The Lowell Observatory at Flagstaff announced the first finding of the planet Pluto.

November 4. With the campaign pledge "Back to prosperity with the Democratic party," former Governor Hunt was re-elected with a solid Democratic legislature.

December 24. In defiance of the law requiring loaves of bread to weigh a pound, small bakers began to produce a 5-cent loaf for the jobless. The courts upheld them ruling the law was invalid.

1931   *March 20.* Governor Hunt vetoed a bill to substitute lethal gas for hanging at the State Penitentiary.

May 18. The U.S. Supreme Court declared the law authorizing construction of Boulder Dam was constitutional in the suit brought by Arizona to stop the building.

1932   *November 9.* Dr. Benjamin B. Moeur, who defeated Hunt in the primary, was elected governor.

December 17. A Federal court jury found that the Indian brew known as "Tiswin" is a sacramental wine and can be legally made on reservations.

1933   *June 26.* Legislature levied tax on retail sales and income.

August 8. By voting, Arizona became the 21st state to sanction the repeal of national prohibition.

October 3. Mrs. Isalolla Greenway was elected Arizona's first woman congressman.

CHRONOLOGY

1933   *October 3.* By referendum, Arizona changed the method of administering capital punishment from hanging to lethal gas.

1934   *January 3.* Congressman Douglas appointed Director of Budget. Mrs. Isalolla S. Greenaway, Ajo, appointed Representative.

March 10. Governor Moeur, fearing California exploitation, ordered Arizona National Guard to prevent erection of Parker Dam.

November 4. Governor Moeur wired the U.S. Department of State that Arizona needed Department of Justice help in handling the anti-alien situation. He said he could not call out the National Guard without the counties' request and none had done so.

November 6. Governor Moeur was re-elected.

November 14. Secretary of the Interior Ickes ordered work stopped on Parker Dam until states' rights had been settled. Governor Moeur withdrew 100 Guardsmen.

1935   *January 21.* The U.S. Supreme Court ruled that Arizona had to show cause why it should not be prohibited from interfering further with work on Parker Dam.

March. The Arizona Senate passed a bill barring aliens from cultivating lands except as day laborers.

April 29. The U.S. Supreme Court reversed its former ruling and held that Arizona owned the east bank of the Colorado.

May 27. Arizona agreed to let California erect Parke Dam, in return for the right to build a dam at

1935 Headgate Rock which would water Colorado Indian Reservation lands, U.S. Senate accepted the compromise.

June 16. The Navajo of Arizona and New Mexico voted to reject the government's offer of home rule.

December 9. The U.S. Supreme Court granted Arizona's plea and gave California until January 15 to show cause why Arizona should not be permitted to petition for a U.S. decree apportioning waters of the Colorado among upper and lower basin states.

1936 *March.* The Arizona Supreme Court upheld the alien land laws.

September 11. President Franklin D. Roosevelt officially opened the giant spill ways of Boulder Dam, the world's highest dam (727 feet).

November 3. R. C. Stanford was elected governor in an election leaving only one Republican in the legislature.

1937 *January 5.* John R. Murdock, Tempe, seated as Representative.

1939 Bartlett Dam, world's highest multiple-arch dam, was completed.

1940 *August.* The Communist party was banned from primary and general elections.

August. The writ sought by the Communist party to compel the Secretary of State to put the party on the primary ballot was denied.

1941 *January 3.* Ernest W. McFarland, Florence, succeeded Senator Ashurst. Sidney P. Osborn became governor.

1942	*November.* Governor Osborn was re-elected.
1944	*November.* Governor Osborn was re-elected.
1946	*November.* The electorate approved the Constitutional amendment to outlaw the closed shop.
1947	*October.* The President's Commission in its report urged suffrage for the Indians.
1948	*May.* Governor Osborn died and Dan E. Garvey became acting governor.
	July. Arizona Supreme Court decided that reservation Indians should be allowed to vote in primaries.
	September. Reservation Indians voted in primaries for the first time.
	November. Garvey elected governor.
1950	*November.* Howard Pyle, Republican, defeated Mrs. A. Frohmiller's bid for the governorship.
	Population: 749,587 persons.
1951	*June.* President Truman signed an amendment to the Arizona Statehood Enabling Act to permit long-term leases on Arizona land to allow for gas pipelines.
1952	*November.* Governor Pyle was re-elected.
	December. The Arizona Supreme Court ruled that the Governor was not the final authority on publication of documents in his possession in settling a 1949 suit by W. R. Matthews against Governor Garvey.
1955	*March.* The boundary dispute with California was settled.

1955	*November*. Ex-Senator McFarland was elected governor.
1956	*November*. Governor McFarland was re-elected.
1958	*November*. Paul J. Fannin elected governor in a Republican sweep. Barry M. Goldwater elected U.S. Senator.
1960	Population: 1,302,161 persons.
1961	*January*. President Kennedy signed a bill approving a compact with Nevada on the Colorado River boundary.
1962	*November*. Governor Fannin was re-elected.
1964	Barry Goldwater, Republican nominee for President, defeated by Lyndon B. Johnson.
1965	*January 5*. Paul J. Fannin elected U.S. Senator, Samuel P. Goddard, Democrat, elected governor.
1966	*February*. A three-judge Federal Court ordered the Legislature reapportioned and changes in two House of Representatives districts.
	April. The U.S. Supreme Court 5-4, ruled the loyalty oath for state employees was unconstitutional because it was vague and rested on the doctrine of guilt by association.
	November. Governor Goddard was defeated in his bid for re-election by J.R. Williams.
1967	*January*. The first Indian elected to the Legislature, L. House, attended the opening session.
1969	*January 5*. Senator Goldwater elected and seated.

1970

March. The U.S. Senate, 50-37, approved the Cooper amendment extending the 1965 Voting Rights Act to Apache County, on the basis of data that under 50% of the voting-age population was registered and voted in the 1968 elections; the law suspended literacy tests and authorized Federal registration activities in such areas, hitherto the South and now extended to parts of six Northern states.

August. The U.S. filed suit in the Supreme Court to force Arizona to comply with the new law lowering the voting age to 18, abolishing literacy tests and modifying residence requirements. Attorney General Mitchell charged some 73,200 citizens, many Spanish speaking, would be denied right to vote if the state law was not overturned.

November 3. Governor Williams re-elected.

December. The U.S. Supreme Court upheld the 18-year-old vote in Federal elections but ruled that Congress acted unconstitutionally when it lowered the age for state and local elections. Arizona, Idaho, Oregon and Texas had filed suit in opposition to the government.

Population: 1,772,482 persons.

BIOGRAPHICAL DIRECTORY

(Names of persons still living, or persons for whom information was incomplete, have been omitted)

ASHURST, Henry F.
  b. Sept. 13, 1874, Winnemucca, Nev.
  d. May 31, 1962, Phoenix, Ariz.
  U. S. Senator, 1913-41

BASHFORD, Coles
  b. Jan. 24, 1816, Putnam County, N. Y.
  d. Apr. 25, 1878, Oakland, Calif.
  Territorial delegate, 1867-69

BEAN, Curtis C.
  b. Jan. 4, 1828, Corroll County, N. H.
  d. Feb. 1, 1904, New York, N. Y.
  Territorial delegate, 1885-87

BRODIE, Alexander
  b. Nov. 13, 1849, Edwards, N. Y.
  d. May 10, 1918, Haddonfield, N. J.
  Governor of territory, 1902-04

CAMERON, Ralph H.
  b. Oct. 21, 1863, Southport, Me.
  d. Feb. 12, 1953, Washington, D. C.
  Territorial delegate, 1909-11
  U. S. Senator, 1921-27

CAMPBELL, John G.
  b. June 25, 1827, Glasgow, Scotland
  d. Dec. 22, 1903, Prescott, Ariz.
  Territorial delegate, 1879-81

FRANKLIN, Benjamin J.
  b. about 1840, Maysville, Ky.
  d. May 8, 1898, Phoenix, Ariz.
  Territorial governor, 1896-97

FREMONT, John C.
  b. Jan. 21, 1813, Savannah, Ga.
  d. July 13, 1890, New York, N. Y.
  Governor of territory, 1878-83

ARIZONA

GOODWIN, John N.
  b. Oct. 18, 1824, S. Berwick, Me.
  d. Apr. 29, 1887, Augusta, Me.
  Governor of territory, 1863-65
  U. S. Representative (Me.), 1861-63, 1865-67
HOYT, John P.
  b. Oct. 6, 1841, near Austinburg, Ohio
  d. Aug. 27, 1926, Seattle, Wash.
  Territorial governor, 1877-78
HUGHES, Louis C.
  b. May 15, 1844, Philadelphia, Pa.
  d. 1900, Tucson, Ariz.
  Governor of territory, 1893-96
IRWIN, John N.
  b. 1847 in Ohio
  d. 1905, Keokuk, Ia.
  Governor of Idaho Terr., 1883
  Governor of territory (Ariz.), 1890-93
KIBBEY, Joseph H.
  b. Mar. 4, 1853, Centreville, Ind.
  d. June 14, 1924, Phoenix, Ariz.
  Governor of territory, 1905-09
McCORD, Myron H.
  b. Nov. 26, 1844, Ceres, Pa.
  d. 1905, Nogales, Ariz.
  U. S. Representative (Wisc.), 1889-91
  Governor of territory, 1897-98
McCORMICK, Robert C.
  b. May 23, 1832, New York, N. Y.
  d. 1901, New York, N. Y.
  Governor of territory, 1866-69
  Territorial delegate, 1869-75
MURPHY, Nathan O.
  b. Oct. 14, 1849, Jefferson, Me.
  d. 1908, Prescott, Ariz.
  Governor of territory, 1892-94, 1898-1907
  Territorial delegate, 1895-97

OURY, Granville H.
  b. Mar. 12, 1825, Abingdon, Va.
  d. Jan. 11, 1891, Tucson, Ariz.
  Confederate territorial delegate, 1862
  Territorial delegate, 1881-85
POSTON, Charles G.
  b. Apr. 20, 1825, Elizabethtown, Ky.
  d. June 24, 1902, Phoenix, Ariz.
  Territorial delegate, 1864-65
SAFFORD, Anson P. K.
  b. Feb. 14, 1830, Hyde Park, Vt.
  d. Dec. 1891, Tarpon Springs, Fla.
  Territorial governor, 1869-77
SLOAN, Richard E.
  b. June 22, 1857, in Ohio
  d. Dec. 14, 1933, Phoenix, Ariz.
  Governor of territory, 1909-12
SMITH, Marcus A.
  b. Jan. 24, 1851, Harrison County, Ky.
  d. Apr. 7, 1924, Washington, D. C.
  Territorial delegate 1887-95, 1897-99, 1901-03,
    1905-09
  U. S. Senator, 1913-21
STEVENS, Hiram S.
  b. Mar. 20, 1832, Weston, Vt.
  d. Mar. 22, 1893, Tucson, Ariz.
  Territorial delegate, 1875-79
TRITLE, Frederick A.
  b. Aug. 7, 1833, near Chambersburg, Pa.
  d. 1906 in Phoenix, Ariz.
  Territorial governor, 1882-85
WILSON, John F.
  b. May 7, 1846, Pulaski, Tenn.
  d. Apr. 7, 1911, Prescott, Ariz.
  Territorial delegate, 1899-1901, 1903-05
WOLFLEY, Lewis
  b. Oct. 8, 1839, Philadelphia, Pa.
  d. Feb. 2, 1910, Los Angeles, Calif.
  Territorial governor, 1889-90

ZULICK, Meyer
  b. June 3, 1839, Philadelphia, Pa.
  d. Mar. 1, 1926, Asbury Park, N. J.
  Territorial governor, 1885-89

OUTLINE OF CONSTITUTION

I. State Boundaries
Sec. 1. Designation of boundaries
Sec. 2. Alteration of state boundaries

II. Declaration of Rights
Sec. 1. Fundamental principles, recurrence to
Sec. 2. Political power; purpose of government
Sec. 3. Supreme law of the land
Sec. 4. Due process of law
Sec. 5. Right of petition and of assembly
Sec. 6. Freedom of speech and press
Sec. 7. Oaths and affirmations
Sec. 8. Right to privacy
Sec. 9. Irrevocable grants of privileges, franchises or immunities
Sec. 10. Self-incrimination; double jeopardy
Sec. 11. Administration of justice
Sec. 12. Liberty of conscience; appropriations for religious purposes prohibited; religious freedom
Sec. 13. Equal privileges and immunities
Sec. 14. Habeas corpus
Sec. 15. Excessive bail; cruel and unusual punishment
Sec. 16. Corruption of blood; forfeiture of estate
Sec. 17. Eminent domain; just compensation for private property taken; public use as judicial question
Sec. 18. Imprisonment for debt
Sec. 19. Bribery or illegal rebating; witnesses; self-incrimination no defense
Sec. 20. Military power subordinate to civil power
Sec. 21. Free and equal elections
Sec. 22. Bailable offenses

Sec. 23. Trial by jury; jury of less than twelve; verdict by nine or more in civil cases; waiver of jury in civil cases
Sec. 24. Rights of accused in criminal prosecutions
Sec. 25. Bills of attainder; ex post facto laws; impairment of contract obligations
Sec. 26. Bearing arms
Sec. 27. Standing army; quartering soldiers
Sec. 28. Treason
Sec. 29. Hereditary emoluments, privileges or powers; perpetuities or entailments
Sec. 30. Indictment or information; preliminary examination
Sec. 31. Damages for death or personal injuries
Sec. 32. Constitutional provisions mandatory
Sec. 33. Reservation of rights
Sec. 34. Industrial pursuits by state and municipal corporations

III. Distribution of Powers

IV. Legislative Department
  1. Initiative and Referendum

Sec. 1. Legislative authority; initiative and referendum
Sec. 2. Penalty for violation of initiative and referendum provisions

  2. Legislature
Sec. 1. Senate; house of representatives; members; apportionment of representatives; compensation; special session
Sec. 2. Qualifications of members of legislature
Sec. 3. Sessions of legislature; special sessions; limitation of subjects for consideration
Sec. 4. Disqualification for membership in legislature
Sec. 5. Ineligibility of members of legislature

OUTLINE OF CONSTITUTION 41

Sec. 6. to other public offices
Privilege from arrest; civil process
Sec. 7. Freedom of debate
Sec. 8. Organization; officers; rules of procedure
Sec. 9. Quorum; compelling attendance; adjournment
Sec. 10. Journal of proceedings; roll call
Sec. 11. Disorderly behavior; expulsion of members
Sec. 12. Procedure on bills; approval or disapproval by governor
Sec. 13. Subject and title of bills
Sec. 14. Legislation by reference prohibited
Sec. 15. Passage of bills by majority; signing of bills
Sec. 16. Right to protest
Sec. 17. Extra compensation prohibited; increase or decrease of compensation during term of office
Sec. 18. Suits against state
Sec. 19. Local or special laws
Sec. 20. Appropriation bills
Sec. 21. Terms of members of legislature
Sec. 22. [Repealed]
Sec. 23. Passes and purchase of transportation by public officers; inapplication to national guard
Sec. 24. Enacting clause of bills; initiative bills

V. Executive Department
Sec. 1. Executive department; state officers; terms; election; residence and office at seat of government; duties
Sec. 2. Eligibility to state offices
Sec. 3. Governor, commander-in-chief of military forces
Sec. 4. Governor; powers and duties; special sessions of legislature; message and

		recommendations
Sec.	5.	Reprieves, commutations and pardons
Sec.	6.	Death, resignation, removal or disability of governor; succession to office; impeachment, absence from state or temporary disability
Sec.	7.	Presentation of bills to governor; approval; veto; filing with secretary of state; veto of items in appropriation bills; inapplication of veto power to referred bills
Sec.	8.	Vacancies in office
Sec.	9.	Powers and duties of state officers
Sec.	10.	Ineligibility of state treasurer to succeed himself
Sec.	11.	Canvass of election returns for state officers; certificates of election
Sec.	12.	Commissions
Sec.	13.	Salaries of state officers

VI. Judicial Department

Sec.	1.	Judicial power; courts
Sec.	2.	Supreme court; composition; divisions; decisions; transaction of business
Sec.	3.	Supreme court; administrative supervision; chief justice
Sec.	4.	Supreme court; election of justices; term of office; vacancies
Sec.	5.	Supreme court; jurisdiction; writs; rules; habeas corpus
Sec.	6.	Supreme court; qualifications of justices
Sec.	7.	Supreme court; clerk and assistants; administrative director and staff
Sec.	8.	Supreme court; publication of opinions
Sec.	9.	Intermediate appellate courts
Sec.	10.	Superior courts; number of judges
Sec.	11.	Superior courts; presiding judges; duties

Sec. 12. Superior courts; election of judges; term of office; vacancies
Sec. 13. Superior courts; composition; salaries; judgments and proceedings; process
Sec. 14. Superior courts; original jurisdiction
Sec. 15. Superior courts; proceedings affecting children
Sec. 16. Superior courts; appellate jurisdiction
Sec. 17. Superior courts; conduct of business; trial juries; jury trial; grand juries
Sec. 18. Superior courts; writs
Sec. 19. Superior courts; service of judge in another county
Sec. 20. Service of retired justices and judges
Sec. 21. Superior courts; speedy decision
Sec. 22. Superior and other courts; qualifications of judges
Sec. 23. Superior courts; clerk
Sec. 24. Superior courts; courts commissioners, masters and referees
Sec. 25. Style of process; conduct of prosecutions in name of state
Sec. 26. Oath of office
Sec. 27. Charge to juries; reversal of causes for technical error
Sec. 28. Justices and judges; dual office holding; practice of law
Sec. 29. Justices and judges; salaries
Sec. 30. Courts of record
Sec. 31. Judges pro tempore
Sec. 32. Justices of the peace and inferior courts; jurisdiction, powers and duties; terms of office; salaries
Sec. 33. Change by legislature in number of justices or judges; reduction of salary during term of office
Sec. 34. Absence of judicial officer from state
Sec. 35. Continuation in office; continued existence of offices; application of prior statute and rules

VII. Suffrage and Elections
Sec. 1. Method of voting; secrecy
Sec. 2. Qualifications of voters; disqualification
Sec. 3. Voting residence of federal employees and certain others
Sec. 4. Privilege of electors from arrest
Sec. 5. Military duty on day of election
Sec. 6. Residence of military personnel stationed within state
Sec. 7. Highest number of votes received as determinative of person elected
Sec. 8. Qualifications for voters at school elections
Sec. 9. Advisory vote
Sec. 10. Direct primary election law
Sec. 11. General elections; date
Sec. 12. Registration and other laws
Sec. 13. Submission of questions upon bond issues or special assessments
Sec. 14. Fee for placing candidate's name on ballot
Sec. 15. Officers to be qualified voters
Sec. 16. Campaign contributions and expenditures; publicity

VIII. Removal from Office
    1. Recall of Officials

Sec. 1. Officers subject to recall; petitioners
Sec. 2. Recall petitions; contents; filing; signatures; oath
Sec. 3. Resignation of officer; special election
Sec. 4. Special election; candidates; results; qualification of successor
Sec. 5. Recall petitions; restrictions and conditions
Sec. 6. Application of general election laws; implementary legislation

OUTLINE OF CONSTITUTION 45

    2. Impeachment
Sec. 1. Power of impeachment in house of representatives; trial by senate
Sec. 2. Conviction; grounds for impeachment; judgment; liability to trial

IX. Public Debt, Revenue, Taxation

Sec. 1. Surrender of power of taxation; uniformity of taxes
Sec. 2. Tax exemptions
Sec. 3. Annual tax; purposes; amount; tax laws; payment of taxes into state treasury
Sec. 4. Fiscal year; annual statement of receipts and expenditures; deficit
Sec. 5. Power of state to contract debts; purposes; limit; restrictions
Sec. 6. Local assessments and taxes
Sec. 7. Gift or loan of credit; subsidies; stock ownership; joint ownership
Sec. 8. Local debt limits; assent of taxpayers
Sec. 9. Statement of tax and objects
Sec. 10. Aid of church, private or sectarian school, or public service corporation
Sec. 11. Taxing procedure; license tax on registered vehicles
Sec. 12. Authority to provide for levy and collection of license and other taxes
Sec. 13. Inventory tax on materials and products of manufacturers
Sec. 14. Use and distribution of vehicle and gasoline tax receipts

X. State and School Lands

Sec. 1. Acceptance and holding of lands by state in trust
Sec. 2. Unauthorized disposition of land or proceeds as breach of trust
Sec. 3. Mortgage or other encumbrance; sale or lease at public auction
Sec. 4. Sale or other disposal; appraisal; minimum price; credit; passing of title
Sec. 5. Minimum price; relinquishment of lands to United States
Sec. 6. Lands reserved by United States for development of water power
Sec. 7. Establishment of funds; receipts; handling
Sec. 8. Conformity of contracts with enabling act
Sec. 9. Sale or lease; conditions; limitations; lease prior to adoption of constitution
Sec. 10. Laws for sale or lease of state lands; protection of residents and lessees
Sec. 11. Maximum acreage allowed single purchaser

XI. Education

Sec. 1. Public school system; establishment and maintenance; elements; education of the deaf, dumb, and blind
Sec. 2. Conduct and supervision of school system
Sec. 3. State board of education; composition; powers and duties; compensation
Sec. 4. State superintendent of public instruction; board membership; powers and duties
Sec. 5. Regents of university and other governing boards; appointment by governor; membership of governor on board of regents
Sec. 6. Admission of students of both sexes to state educational institutions; tuition; common school system

Sec. 7. Sectarian instruction; religious or political test or qualification
Sec. 8. Permanent state school fund source; apportionment of income to counties
Sec. 9. County school fund; size of fund; free schools
Sec. 10. Source of revenue for maintenance of state educational institutions

XII. Counties
Sec. 1. Counties as bodies politic and corporate
Sec. 2. Counties of territory as counties of state
Sec. 3. County officers; election; term of office
Sec. 4. County officers; duties, powers, and qualifications; salaries

XIII. Municipal Corporations
Sec. 1. Incorporation and organization; classification
Sec. 2. Charter; preparation and proposal by board of freeholders; ratification and approval; amendment
Sec. 3. Election of board of freeholders
Sec. 4. Franchises; approval of electors; term
Sec. 5. Right of municipal corporation to engage in business or enterprise
Sec. 6. Franchises; restrictions
Sec. 7. Irrigation and other districts as political subdivisions

XIV. Other Corporations
Sec. 1. Corporation defined; right to sue and suability

Sec. 2. Formation under general laws;
change of laws; regulation
Sec. 3. Existing charters
Sec. 4. Restriction to business
authorized by charter or law
Sec. 5. Foreign corporations; transaction of business
Sec. 6. Stocks; bonds
Sec. 7. Lease or alienation of franchise
Sec. 8. Filing of articles of incorporation;
place of business; agent for service of process; venue
Sec. 9. Eminent domain; taking corporate
property and franchises for public
use
Sec. 10. Elections for directors or managers
Sec. 11. Liability of stockholders
Sec. 12. Officers of banking institutions;
individual responsibility
Sec. 13. Want of legal organization as a
defense
Sec. 14. Legislative power to impose
conditions
Sec. 15. Monopolies and trusts
Sec. 16. Records, books, and files;
visitorial and inquisitorial
powers of state
Sec. 17. Fees; reports; licensing of
foreign corporations
Sec. 18. Contributions to influence election
or official action
Sec. 19. Penalties for violation of article

XV. Corporation Commission
Sec. 1. Composition; election; term of
office; office and residence;
vacancies; qualifications
Sec. 2. Public service corporation defined

OUTLINE OF CONSTITUTION 49

Sec. 3. Power of commission as to classifications, rates and charges, rules contracts, and accounts; local regulation
Sec. 4. Power to inspect and investigate
Sec. 5. Power to issue certificates of incorporation and licenses
Sec. 6. Enlargement of powers by legislature; rules and regulations
Sec. 7. Connecting and intersecting lines of transportation and communications corporations
Sec. 8. Transportation by connecting carriers
Sec. 9. Transmission of messages by connecting carriers
Sec. 10. Railways as public highways; railroad and other corporations as common carriers
Sec. 11. Movable property as personal property; liability of property to attachment, execution and sale
Sec. 12. Charges for service; discrimination; free or reduced rate transportation
Sec. 13. Reports to commission
Sec. 14. Value of property of public service corporations
Sec. 15. Acceptance of constitutional provisions by existing corporations
Sec. 16. Forfeitures for violations
Sec. 17. Appeal to courts
Sec. 18. Salary of commissioners; expenses
Sec. 19. Power to impose fines

XVI. Militia
Sec. 1. Composition of militia
Sec. 2. Composition and designation of organized militia
Sec. 3. Conformity to federal regulations

XVII. Water Rights
Sec. 1. Riparian water rights
Sec. 2. Recognition of existing rights

XVIII. Labor
Sec. 1. Eight-hour day
Sec. 2. Child labor
Sec. 3. Contractual immunity of employer from liability for negligence
Sec. 4. Fellow servant doctrine
Sec. 5. Contributory negligence and assumption of risk
Sec. 6. Recovery of damages for injuries
Sec. 7. Employer's liability law
Sec. 8. Workmen's compensation law
Sec. 9. Blacklists
Sec. 10. Employment of aliens

XIV. Mines
Par. 1. Toleration of religious sentiment
Par. 2. Polygamy
Par. 3. Introduction of intoxicating liquors into Indian country
Par. 4. Public lands; Indian lands
Par. 5. Taxation
Par. 6. Territorial debts and liabilities
Par. 7. Public school system; suffrage
Par. 8. English language
Par. 9. Location of state capital
Par. 10. [Repealed]
Par. 11. [Repealed]
Par. 12. Lands granted to state
Par. 13. Ordinance as part of constitution; amendment

XX. Ordinance
Sec. 1. Introduction in legislature;
         initiative petition; election
Sec. 2. Convention

XXI. Mode of Amending
Sec. 1. Existing rights, actions, suits,
         proceedings, contracts, claims, or
         demands; process
Sec. 2. Territorial laws
Sec. 3. Debts, fines, penalties, and
         forfeitures
Sec. 4. Recognizances; bonds; estate;
         judgments; choses in action
Sec. 5. Criminal prosecutions and penal
         actions; offenses; penalties, actions
         and suits
Sec. 6. Territorial, district, county, and
         precinct officers
Sec. 7. Causes pending in district courts of
         territory; records, papers, and
         property
Sec. 8. Probate records and proceedings
Sec. 9. Causes pending in supreme court
         of territory; records, papers, and
         property
Sec. 10. Seals of supreme court, superior
         courts, municipalities, and county
         officers
Sec. 11. Effective date of constitution
Sec. 12. Election of representative in
         congress
Sec. 13. Continuation in office until
         qualification of successor
Sec. 14. Initiative
Sec. 15. Public institutions
Sec. 16. Confinement of minor offenders

Sec. 17. Compensation of public officers
Sec. 18. State examiner
Sec. 19. Lobbying
Sec. 20. Design of state seal
Sec. 21. Enactment of laws to carry constitution into effect
Sec. 22. Judgments of death

SELECTED DOCUMENTS

Arizona, and its neighboring Southwestern states, are firmly fixed in the American mind as the lingering preserve of the Old West. It seemed appropriate, therefore, to select documents for this state which reflected the Old West in the eyes of contemporaries, as illustrating the heritage. In some instances, the documents are reproduced from the original printed source to add to the flavor of the writing.

J. Ross Brown, one of a group of artists who traveled in the American West in the frontier era to preserve in pen and brush sketches the things they witnessed, prepared an illustrated volume published by Harper and Brothers in New York in 1869 under the title, *Adventures in the Apache Country*. His description of the Arizona territory is a natural stage for the "true confession" article written by an early prototype of the Bonnie of Bonnie and Clyde -- Pearl Hart, a woman bandit whose story, perhaps ghost-written, appeared in *Cosmopolitan Magazine* in October 1899. The image of the Old West was fixed in these writings; in January 1906 the journalist Michael G. Cunniff in *World's Work* could advise the eastern reader that "The Last of the Territories" was ready for conventional statehood. But the frontier had made a lasting impact upon American political thought; it was in the West that Populist reform assumed the most radical proportions, and William Howard Taft vetoed the first Arizona statehood bill because of the provision for recall of judges. The final documents, appropriately enough, deal with his reasoning and the comment upon it.

ADVENTURES IN THE APACHE COUNTRY

John Ross Browne

(John Ross Browne, 1821-1875, was one of a group of artists and writers, of whom John James Audubon, 1785-1851, was the archtype, who traveled throughout the New World and reported their contemporary observations to a wide readership on the Eastern seaboard and in Europe. Irish-born Browne was already a world traveler and well-known writer and artist before he ventured into the American Southwest in the mid-1860's. He was for a number of years a regular contributor to Harper's New Monthly Magazine, *and had written several books on his travels in Europe, Africa and the Pacific islands.*

*(*Adventures in the Apache Country: A Tour Through Arizona and Sonora, *was published by Harper's in 1869. On the following pages appear the reprints of his chapters on several sites and experiences in the Arizona territory in the first twenty years after its acquisition by the United States.)*

DOCUMENTS
Across the Ninety-Mile Desert.

SKETCHING in Arizona is rather a ticklish pursuit. I shall not readily forget my experience of the canyons and thickets, and the queer feeling produced by the slightest sound that fell upon my ears as I hurriedly committed the outlines to paper. It has been my fortune to furnish the world with sketches of Madagascar, Zanzibar, Palestine, the Continent of Europe, Iceland, and some few other points, many of which were achieved under circumstances of peculiar difficulty; but I never before travelled through a country in which I was compelled to pursue the fine arts with a revolver strapped around my body, a double-barreled shot-gun lying across my knees, and half a dozen soldiers armed with Sharpe's carbines keeping guard in the distance. Even with all the safeguards of pistols and soldiers I am free to admit that on occasions of this kind I frequently looked behind to see how the country appeared in its rear aspect. An artist with an arrow in his back may be a very picturesque object to contemplate at one's leisure; but I would rather draw him on paper than sit for the portrait myself. All the way up from Fort Yuma I was beset by these difficulties; and if any man of genius and enterprise thinks he could do better under the circumstances he is welcome to try.

At Sacatone we had a grand pow-wow with the Pimo chiefs. Antonio Azul and his interpreter, Francisco, had apprised the nation of the munificent presents that we had for distribution. Great was the sensation throughout the Pimeria. Scarcely had the sun risen above the scraggy brush of the desert when the dusky chiefs, head-men and people came pouring in. They came from the river-bottom, from the villages, from the weeds, from the grass, and possibly from the holes in the ground. On horseback and on foot they came; by twos and by threes, and by sixes and by dozens. Paint and red blankets, beads and brass buttons, shone with resplendent brilliancy around our encampment. By noon it presented a busy scene of savage enjoyment. The Pimo belles were in their glory. Plump and good-natured; their pretty eyes fringed around with black paint; their teeth shining in pearly whiteness; their bosoms bare; their forms of almost Grecian symmetry and delicacy. Poston, with his enthusiastic appreciation of beauty, would have lost his balance completely had I not warned him of the dangers that surrounded him; so that when severely pressed by a bevy of Pimo maidens for beads, calicoes, and the like, he usually closed both his eyes and handed out the presents at random. In this way I observed that he frequently gave a sash, or shawl, or or string of beads to some stalwart buck, and a shovel or pickaxe to some tender maid. When the looking-glasses and tin jewelry were distributed, never was there such a sensation in Pimeria; and as for the fancy calicoes, the excitement produced by the sight of them can not but descend to the Pimo posterity, and the name of Mr. Commissioner Dole be blessed unto the last generation of these good people. I have no doubt many of them will name their children Dole. I conscientiously believe that historians in future ages will find the name of Dole common among the Pimos. My friend Poston made a speech to Antonio Azul that in point of metaphor and eloquence has never, I venture to assert, been surpassed in this region of country.

Availing ourselves of the friendly professions made by the chiefs and people, we signified that two pumpkins for our journey across the desert would be a most acceptable return for the laborious services we had rendered the great cause of civilization;

whereupon over a dozen pumpkins were immediately dragged forth from the loose and somewhat discolored drapery that hung around the squaws. We gracefully thanked them and proceeded to pick up our vegetables. "Dos reals," said the Indians. We gave them two bits. "Quatro reals," they observed. We offered them four bits. They gravely wrapped up their pumpkins. We offered a dollar for two. They coolly demanded two dollars. We indignantly showed them the way out of camp. Antonio and Francisco had long since disappeared before the impending storm. Not so their followers, who, in this case, were no followers at all. Firmly as rocks of adamant they sat gossiping upon the ground, regardless of our displeasure. Some of them considered it in the light of a friendly invitation to supper, and hung about the fire snuffing the odorous fumes of the pots and frying-pans. Toward the shades of evening the pumpkin-venders had sufficiently warmed their backs and were about to depart. Our cook, Dr. Berry, was in favor of seizing a choice pair of pumpkins as a military necessity, but that proposition was overruled as beneath the dignity of our official position. Have them, however, we must. They were indispensable to our health. I left it all to Poston, whom I knew to possess a high order of genius for trade. He traded for two hours; he was calm and violent by turns; he reasoned and raved alternately. I fell asleep. When I awoke, triumph sat perched upon his brow. The Indians were gone. Success had crowned his efforts. Two pumpkins, the spoils of victory, lay at his feet. "What did they cost?" was my natural inquiry. He looked a little confused, but quickly rallied, and replied, "Oh, not much - for this country! Let me see - five, ten, eighteen, twenty-two. Only about twenty-two dollars in trade."

It was gratifying at all events to know that the Pimos were rapidly becoming a civilized people.

Under these circumstances we thought it advisable to pursue our journey without further waste of time.

Travelling all day from Sacatone we reached the Blue-Water Wells early in the evening, where we camped till dark. A few hours of night-travel brought us to the Pecacho, a little beyond which we made a dry camp till morning. The country between the Gila River and Tucson is a hard, gravelly desert, partially covered with a scrubby growth of mesquit and cactus, and at this season destitute of water except at two or three points, where the wells dug by the Overland Mail Company still remain. In former years emigrant parties suffered much in crossing this inhospitable desert. At certain seasons of the year some pools of water near the Pecacho afford relief to the trains, and enable the emigrants to reach the Gila; but these are a very uncertain dependence.

The Pecacho lies forty-five miles from the Gila, and is about the same distance from Tucson. It presents a prominent and picturesque landmark from both points, and is seen at a great distance from the Papagoria. The name is Spanish, and signifies "point," or "peak." Some travellers have discovered in this curious formation of rocks some resemblance to an axe-head. There are many Pecachos throughout Arizona. I have been unable to see in any of them the most remote resemblance to an axe-head. Generally they consist of two sharp-pointed rocks, one of a triangular and the other of a rectangular shape, growing out of the top of some isolated mountain, and serve to indicate the routes across the desert, which would otherwise be difficult to find.

Tucson.

I HAD no idea before my visit to Arizona that there

existed within the territorial limits of the United
States a city more remarkable in many respects than
Jericho - the walls of which were blown down by horns;
for, in this case, the walls were chiefly built up by
horns - a city realizing, to some extent, my impres-
ssions of what Sodom and Gomorrah must have been before they were destroyed by the vengeance of the Lord.
It is gratifying to find that travel in many lands
has not yet fatally impaired my capacity for receiv-
ing new sensations. Virginia City came near it; but
it was reserved for the city of Tucson to prove that
the world is not yet exhausted of its wonders.

   A journey across the Ninety-mile Desert prepares
the jaded and dust-covered traveller to enjoy all the
luxuries of civilization which an ardent imagination
may lead him to expect in the metropolis of Arizona.
Passing the Point of the Mountain, eighteen miles
below, he is refreshed during the remainder of the
way by scraggy thickets of mesquit, bunches of sage
and grease-wood, beds of sand and thorny cactus; from
which he emerges to find himself on the verge of the
most wonderful scatteration of human habitations his
eye ever beheld - a city of mud-boxes, dingy and dilap-
idated, cracked and baked into a composite of dust
and filth; littered about with broken corrals, sheds,
bake-ovens, carcasses of dead animals, and broken
pottery; barren of verdure, parched, naked, and grim-
ly desolate in the glare of a southern sun. Adobe
walls without whitewash inside or out, hard earth-
floors, baked and dried Mexicans, sore-backed burros,
coyote dogs, and terra-cotta children; soldiers, team-
sters, and honest miners lounging about the mescal-
shops, soaked with the fiery poison; a noisy band of
Sonoranian buffoons, dressed in theatrical costume,
cutting their antics in the public places to the most
diabolical din of fiddles and guitars ever heard; a
long train of Government wagons preparing to start for
Fort Yuma or the Rio Grande - these are what the

traveller sees, and a great many things more, but in vain he looks for a hotel or lodging-house. The best accommodations he can possibly expect are the dried mud walls of some unoccupied outhouse, with a mud floor for his bed; his own food to eat, and his own cook to prepare it; and lucky is he to possess such luxuries as these. I heard of a blacksmith, named Burke, who invited a friend to stop awhile with him at Tucson. Both parties drank whisky all day for occupation and pleasure. When bedtime came, Burke said, "Let's go home and turn in." He led the way up to the Plaza, and began to hand off his clothes. "What are you doing?" inquired his guest. "Going to bed," said Burke-"this is where I gen'rally sleep." And they both turned in on the Plaza, which if hard was at least well-aired and roomy. The stranger started for the Rio Grande the next day.

For various reasons Tucson has long enjoyed an extensive reputation. Before the acquisition of Arizona by the United States the Mexicans had a military post at this place, with a small command for the protection of the missions and adjoining grain fields against the Apaches. It then numbered some four or five hundred souls. Since 1854 it has been the principal town in the Territory, and has been occupied successively by the Federal and rebel troops.

As the centre of trade with the neighboring State of Sonora, and lying on the high-road from the Rio Grande to Fort Yuma, it became during the few years preceding the "break-up" quite a place of resort for traders, speculators, gamblers, horse-thieves, murderers, and vagrant politicians. Men who were no longer permitted to live in California found the climate of Tucson congenial to their health. If the world were searched over I suppose there could not be found so degraded a set of villains as then formed the principal society of Tucson. Every man went armed to the teeth, and street-fights and bloody affrays were of daily occurrence. Since the coming of the California Volunteers, two years ago, the state of things in this delightful metropolis has materially changed. The citizens who are permitted to live here at all still live very much in the Greaser style - the tenantable houses having been taken away from them for the use of the officers and soldiers who are protecting their property from the Apaches. But then, they have claims for rent, which they can probably sell for something when anybody comes along disposed to deal in that sort of paper. Formerly they were troubled a good deal about the care of their cattle and sheep: now they have no trouble at all; the cattle and sheep have fallen into the hands of Apaches, who have become unusually bold in their depredations; and the pigs which formerly roamed unmolested about the streets during the day, and were deemed secure in the backyards of nights, have become a military necessity. Eggs are scarce, because the hens that used to lay them cackle no more in the hen form. Drunkenness has been effectually prohibited by a written order limiting the sale of spirituous liquors to three specific establishments, the owners of which pay a license for hospital purposes, the fund whereof goes to the benefit of the sick and disabled who have fallen a sacrifice to their zeal in the pursuit of hostile Indians. Gambling is also much discountenanced; and nobody gambles when he is out of money, or can't borrow from any other sources. The public regulations are excellent. Volunteer soldiers are stationed all over the town - at the mescal-shops, the monte-tables, and houses of ill-fame - for the preservation of public order, or go there of their own accord for that purpose, which amounts to the same thing. Public property is eminently secure. The Commissary's storehouse is secured by a padlock on the door and a guard in front with a musket on his shoulder; so that nobody can go in at any time of the day or night and steal one hundred pounds of coffee and one hundred pounds of sugar, deposited there by private parties for safe-keeping, without killing the guard and breaking open the padlock, or cutting a hole through the adobe wall. If such a thing did occur it would be considered a reflection upon the entire post, and the loss would at once be reimbursed either from public or private sources. Otherwise people would naturally think very strange of such an occurrence.

Although there are two companies of able-bodied men well-armed and equipped at Tucson, and although the Apaches range within three miles of the place, there is no apprehension felt for the public safety. Citizens in small parties of five or six go out whenever occasion requires, and afford aid and comfort to unfortunate travellers who happen to be waylaid in pursuit of their legitimate business; and the Papago Indians also do good service by following up and killing the hostile savages who infest the country. It is confidently believed, therefore, that as long as the troops are kept within the precincts of the ancient Pueblo of Tucson, they will not be molested by any enemy of a more deadly character than mescal, against which the regulations provide a remedy, and if they don't the physician of the post is prepared to do so free of compensation for eighteen months. Neither can the pangs of starvation assail this important stronghold, unless the climate should unfit them for the heavy labor of lifting the food to their mouths; for, unlike the poor wretches of miners and traders who are prowling around the country in search of a living, the troops here stationed receive their regular salary and rations, and the Government liberally provides them with clothing, medicines, and all they require, and vast numbers of wagons and mules to haul the same from distant points. Besides, there are private traders always ready to furnish them with food from Sonora at a reduction upon the present cost

to Government; and even if none of these sources
could be relied upon, there are abudant tracts of
rich arable lands lying within a few miles, upon which
it would be mere pastime for the men to raise fifty or
sixty bushels of wheat or corn to the acre at an extra
compensation of fifty cents per day - convenient
places where the Papagoes would be willing to protect
them from the Apaches for the trifling consideration
of a few strings of beads or yards of manta. I say,
therefore, there is no reason to apprehend that the
command at Tucson will ever be reduced to the humiliating necessity of depending upon the Pimo Indians who
live on the Gila River for wheat upon which to feed
their mules, to the exclusion of miners, traders, and
other human beings engaged in developing the resources
of the country, whose appetites may crave the same
sort of sustenance, and who, under the ordinary rules
of trade, may come in competition with them, or offer
more to the Indians for the products of their labor.
Such a degradation could never befall California Volunteers. Far rather would they go to work and raise
wheat for their mules, or let the mules die, than
squabble over a miserable pittance of wheat raised by
the industry of a degenerate race, whom they are expected to elevate by their example to the standard of
civilization; nor would they undertake to evade the
imputation that would rest upon them for such an act
by placing it on the ground of military necessity,
when such necessity, if it existed at all, could only
have arisen from negligence, incompetency, or dishon-
esty in their own departments, and which, at all
events, would be a very dangerous plea to establish
in a Territory remote from the seat of rebellion, and
under the acknowledged protection of civil law. By
proclamation of the Governor, and by orders of the
commanding officer of the department, declaring that
martial law no longer prevailed, and that the military
should afford all the aid in their power in carrying

the civil law into effect, such a mortifying state of things is expressly provided against.

News reached us at this place of the massacre by the Apaches of two gentlemen well known to the members of our party - Mr. J. B. Mills, Superintendent of the Patagonia Mines, and Mr. Edwin Stevens, who had just come down by the way of Guvamas to take his place; also of an attack by the same band of Indians upon Mr. S. F. Butterworth, President of the Arizona Mining Company. The statements were conflicting, and there were still some members of Mr. Butterworth's party for whose safety great anxiety was felt. As our route lay in part through the same region of country in which these startling events had taken place, we made immediate application for an escort from the detachment who had accompanied us from Fort Yuma, in the hope of being enabled to render some assistance to our friends.

A sojourn of two or three days quite satisfied us with the metropolis of Arizona. It is a very delightful place for persons of elegant leisure; but as we belonged to the class who are compelled to labor for a living, there was no excuse for our staying beyond the time necessary to complete arrangements for our tour through the silver regions of the South.

From which it will at once be seen that Tucson has greatly improved within the past two years, and offers at the present time rare attractions for visitors from all parts of the world, including artists, who can always find in it subjects worthy of their genius. The views of life, the varied attitudes of humanity that I, a mere sketcher, found in the purlieus of the town as well as in public places, will be valuable to posterity; but, as Dr. Johnson said when looking from an eminence over the road that led out of Scotland into England, it was the finest view he had seen in the country, so I must be permitted to say the best view of Tucson is the rear view on the road to Fort Yuma.

On the 19th of January we set forth on our journey with an escort of thirty men belonging to Company G, California Volunteers, under command of Lieutenant Arnold. I may here be allowed to say that a better set of men I never travelled with. They were good-humored, obliging, and sober, and not one of them stole a pig or a chicken during the entire trip.

San Xavier Del Bac.

NINE miles from Tucson we came to the fine old mission of San Xavier del Bac, built by the Jesuits in 1668. This is one of the most beautiful and picturesque edifices of the kind to be found on the North American continent. I was surprised to see such a splendid monument to civilization in the wilds of Arizona. The front is richly ornamented with fanciful decorations in masonry; a lofty bell-tower rises at each corner, one of which is capped by a dome; the other still remains in an unfinished condition. Over the main chapel in the rear is also a large dome; and the walls are surmounted by massive cornices and ornaments appropriately designed. The material is principally brick, made, no doubt, on the spot. The style of architecture is Saracenic. The entire edifice is perfect in the harmony of its proportions. In every point of view the eye is satisfied. Mr. Mowry well observes, in his pamphlet on Arizona, that, "incredible as it may seem, the church of San Xavier, with its elaborate facade, its dome and spires, would today be an ornament to the architecture of New York."

A village of Papago Indians, numbering some two or three hundred souls, partially surrounds the mission. There are also a few Mexicans living among the Indians; but they are regarded with distrust, and complaint is made that they have intruded themselves against the wish of the tribe. Mr. Poston, upon investigation of the matter, ordered the Mexicans to leave.

As far back as our knowledge of the Papagoes extends they have been a peaceable, industrious, and friendly race. They live here, as they lived two centuries ago, by cultivating the low grounds in the vicinity, which they make wonderfully productive by a system of irrigation. Wheat, corn, pumpkins, and pomegranates are the principal articles os subsistence raised by these Indians; and they seem to enjoy an abundance of every thing necessary for health and comfort. They profess the Catholic faith, and are apparently sincere converts. The Jesuit missionaries taught them those simple forms which they retain to this day, though of late years they have been utterly neglected. The women sing in the church with a degree of sweetness and harmony that quite surprised me. At the time of our visit two Padres from Santa Clara, California, who had come as far as Tucson with the command, had just taken up their qurters in the mission. From my acquaintance with them on the road, I judge them to be very sincere and estimable as well as intelligent men. We furnished them with a Pimo grammar, published by Mr. Buckingham Smith, late American Secretary of Legation to Spain, and they are now studying that language with a view of holding more advantageous intercourse with the Papagoes, who are originally a branch of the Pimos, and speak the same language. The reverend fathers entertained us during our sojourn with an enthusiastic account of their plans for the restoration of the mission and the instruction and advancement of the Indian tribes, with whom they were destined to be associated for some years to come.

Subject as the Papagoes are to frequent encroachments from the Apaches, they are compelled to keep their cattle closely watched. At present they possess scarcely sufficient stock for the ordinary purposes of agriculture. Not more than five or six months ago a small band of Apaches made a foray within a mile of the village, and carried away with them at a single swoop most of the stock then grazing in the pastures. Though naturally disposed to peaceful pursuits, the Papagoes are not deficient in courage. On one occasion, when the principal chiefs and braves were away gathering *patayah* in the desert, the old men and boys of the tribe kept at bay, and finally beat off, a band of over two hundred Apaches who made a descent upon the village. Frequently they pursue their hereditary enemies to the mountains, and in almost every engagement inflict upon them a severe chastisement.

Leaving San Xavier, we followed the course of the Santa Cruz Valley for two days, making only one camp at Rhodes's ranch. I had supposed, previous to our entrance into this region, that Arizona was nearly a continuous desert, as indeed it is from Fort Yuma to Tucson; but nothing can be a greater mistake than to form a general opinion of the country from a journey up the Gila. The valley of the Santa Cruz is one of the richest and most beautiful grazing and agricultural regions I have ever seen. Occasionally the river sinks, but even at these points the grass is abundant and luxuriant. We travelled, league after league, through waving fields of grass, from two to four feet high, and this at a season when cattle were dying of starvation all over the middle and southern parts of California. Mesquit and cotton-wood are abundant, and there is no lack of water most of the way to Santa Cruz.

Three years ago this beautiful valley was well settled by an enterprising set of frontiersmen as far up as the Calabasas ranch, fifteen miles beyond Tubac. At the breaking out of the rebellion, when the Overland Stage Line was withdrawn, the whole Territory, as stated in a previous chapter, went to ruin with a rapidity almost unparalleled. The Apaches, supposing they had created a panic among the whites, became more bold and vigorous in their forays than ever. Ranch after ranch was desolated by fire, robbery, and murder. No white man's life was secure beyond Tucson; and even there the few inhabitants lived in a state of terror.

I saw on the road between San Xavier and Tubac, a distance of forty miles, almost as many graves of the white men murdered by the Apaches within the past few years. Literally the road-side was marked with the burial-places of these unfortunate settlers. There is not now a single living soul to enliven the solitude. All is silent and death-like; yet strangely calm and beautiful in its desolation. Here were fields with torn-down fences; houses burned or racked to pieces by violence, the walls cast about in heaps over the once-pleasant homes; everywhere ruin, grim and ghastly with associations of sudden death. I have rarely travelled through a country more richly favored, yet more depressing in its associations with the past. Day and night the common subject of conversation was murder; and wherever our attention was attracted by the beauty of the scenery or the richness of the soil a stone-covered grave marked the foreground.

The history of Bill Rhodes, at whose ranch we camped, was an example. In the full tide of success this daring frontiersman returned to his house one evening, and found his comrades murdered and himself surrounded by a large band of Apaches. By some means he managed to break through their lines; but his horse being jaded it soon became apparent that escape was impossible. Just as the pursuing Indians were upon him he flung himself into a willow thicket and there made battle. A circle was formed around him by the blood-stained and yelling devils, who numbered at least thirty; but he was too cool a man to be intimidated by their infernal demonstrations. For three hours he kept them at bay with his revolver; although they poured into the thicket an almost continuous volley of rifle-shots and arrows. A ball struck him in the left arm, near the elbow, and nearly disabled him from loss of blood. He buried the wounded part in the sand and continued the fight till the Indians, exasperated at his stubborn resistance, rushed up in a body, determined to put an end to him at once. He had but two shots left. With one of these he killed the first Indian that approached, when the rest whirled about and stood off. They then addressed him in Spanish, calling him by name, and telling him he was a brave man, and if he would come out they would spare his life. "No," said he, "d--n you! I'll kill the last one of you before you shall take me!" He had given such good evidence of his ability in that way that they held a parley and concluded he was about right; so they retired and left him master of the field. Bill Rhodes's Apache fight is now one of the standard incidents in the history of Arizona.

Pueblo of Tubac.

ON reaching the old Pueblo of Tubac we found that we were the only inhabitants. There was not a living soul to be seen as we approached. The old Plaza was knee-deep with weeds and grass. All around were adobe houses, with the roofs fallen in and the walls crumbling to ruin. Door and windows were all gone, having been carried away by the Mexicans three years ago. Old pieces of machinery belonging to the neighboring mines lay scattered about the main building, formerly the headquarters of the Arizona Mining Company. Many of these are still valuable. At the time of the abandonment of the country in 1861, the Arizona Company had upward of $60,000 worth of machinery stored in the building attached to the old tower, every pound of which was hauled in wagons at great expense from Lavaca in Texas, a distance of twelve hundred miles. Two boilers, weighing 6000 pounds each, were hauled in the same way, one of which was taken by the Patagonia Mining Company. The other, at the time of our journey, lay on the Sonora road a little beyond the Calabasas. Some Mexicans were hauling it away when they were attacked by a band of Apaches, who killed two of the party, took the teams, burned the wagon, and left the boiler on the roadside, where it lay when we passed.

Tubac was first settled by the Americans in 1856, when my friend Poston, the Arizona pioneer and late superintending agent of the silver mines in this vicinity, established it as his headquarters. It lies on a pleasant slope in one of the most beautiful parts of the valley of the Santa Cruz, within twelve miles of the Santa Rita silver mines, and about twenty-two from the Heintzelman or Cerro Colorado, two of the richest mining districts within the limits of the Territory. Under the direction of Mr. Poston, Tubac was soon partially rebuilt. Good houses and store-rooms were erected, old buildings were repaired; a farm was fenced in and put under cultivation; a fine garden was started and irrigated by acequias in the Mexican style; and it may literally be said "the wilderness blossomed as the rose." In 1858, '59, and '60, during which the mines were in progress of development, Tubac might well be regarded as the headquarters of civilization in the Territory. Men of refinement and education connected with the mines were here occasionally assembled, and even the fair sex was well represented. The gardens afforded a pleasant place of retreat in summer, with their shady groves of acacias and peach-trees; and deep pools in the river, overhung by willows, were cleared out and made into bathing-places, in which all who pleased might refresh themselves with a luxurious bath. Poston used to sit in the water, like the Englishman in Hyperion, and read the newspapers, by which means he kept his temper cool amid the various disturbing influences that surrounded him.

Tubac is now a city of ruins - ruin and desolation wherever the eye rests. Yet I can not but believe that the spirit of American enterprise will revisit this delightful region, and re-establish, on a more permanent footing, all that has been lost, and as much more as its enterprising American founder conceived in his most sanguine anticipations. The mines are proverbially rich; and rich mines will sooner or later secure the necessary protection for working them. A view of the Plaza, and especially the old tower upon which, amid the cheers of our escort, we planted the glorious flag of our Union, will convey some idea of the general character of the town.

As a matter of historical interest, characteristic of the vicissitudes suffered by these border towns of Arizona, a few incidents connected with the depopulation of Tubac will not be deemed out of place. In 1840, according to Valesquez, the post was garrisoned by thirty men, and the town contained a population of four hundred. After the boundary-line was established and the Mexican troops were withdrawn, the entire population retired to Santa Cruz, Imuriz, Magdalena, and other points within the Sonora line. Subsequently, when it became the headquarters of the Arizona Mining Company, it contained a mixed population of four or five hundred, consisting of Americans, Germans, Mexican peons, and Indians. When the Federal troops were withdrawn to the Rio Grande, Tubac was again partially abandoned, only twenty-five or thirty souls remaining. At this period (1861) the Apaches came down from the mountains in large force, and surrounded the town with a view of plundering it; but the few Americans left made a bold defense, and kept them at bay for several days, although it is estimated they numbered over two hundred. The beleaguered residents, finding they would ultimately be overwhelmed or starved out, sent an express to Tucson during the night, stating their condition and asking for assistance. A brave and generous American, Mr. Grant Ourey, got up a party of twenty-five men, and by rapid and skillful movements came suddenly upon the Apaches, whom they attacked with such spirit that the whole band fled in a panic to the Santa Rita mountains. At the time of Mr. Ourey's arrival a party of seventy-five Mexicans, who had heard that the Government of the United States was broken up, came in from Sonora with the same purpose of plunder which the Apaches had just attempted to carry into effect. Seeing the preparations for defense they fell back upon Tumacacari, three miles distant, where an old American lived, whom even the Apaches had spared, killed him in cold blood, robbed the place of all it contained worth carrying away, and retired to Sonora. Thus harassed on both sides by Apaches and Mexicans, and without hope of future protection, the inhabitants of Tubac for the last time abandoned the town; and thus it has remained ever since, a melancholy spectacle of ruin and desolation.

We were exceedingly anxious to discover some trace of our American friends who had recently suffered such a disastrous attack from the Indians - especially of Messrs. Kustel, Janin, and Higgins, who had crossed over from the Patagonia mines, and of whose safety we had no intelligence. There was abundant reason to suppose they had fallen into the hands of the same band of Apaches who had killed Mr. Mills and Mr. Stevens and robbed Mr. Butterworth. Our vaquero discovered fresh traces of a wagon on the Santa Rita road, which somewhat re-assured us of their safety; but we were not yet satisfied. It was deemed advisable under the circumstances to send the vaquero with a detachment of five men over to the Santa Rita hacienda, with instructions to make a careful examination of the premises, and join us the next day at Calabasas. As an instance of the wonderful sagacity of the Mexicans in determining the number and movements of parties entirely unknown to them, from signs which to us would be quite unintelligible, the vaquero reported next day that he had found traces of our American friends. He stated the number exactly; gave many curious particulars in regard to their movements, and said we had missed them by eight days. Nor was there any mere conjecture about this information. It was all demonstrated by the closest reasoning upon isolated and trifling yet incontrovertible signs; and what is most remarkable, his statement was subsequently corroborated by the facts in every particular.

We killed several deer in the vicinity of Tubac, which contributed materially to our scanty stock of provisions. Wild turkeys were also abundant, but our hunters failed to get a shot at them, although their tracks were to be seen within a stone's throw of the Plaza.

Leaving a written notice upon the wall of the old fort, informing all persons who might pass this way of our arrival and departure, we proceeded without loss of time on our journey.

Three miles beyond Tubac we made a halt to visit the old mission of San Jose de Tumacacari, another of those interesting relics of Jesuit enterprise which abound in this country. The mission lies a little to the right of the road, and is pleasantly situated on a slope, within a few hundred yards of the Santa Cruz River. A luxuriant growth of cotton-wood, mesquit, and shrubbery of various kinds, fringes the bed of the river and forms a delightful shade from the heat of the sun, which even in midwinter has something of a summer glow about it. Like San Xavier and other missions built by the Jesuits, Tumacacari is admirably situated for agricultural purposes. The remains of acequias show that the surrounding valley lands must have been at one time in a high state of cultivation. Broken fences, ruined out-buildings, bakehouses, corrals, etc., afford ample evidence that the old Jesuits were not deficient in industry. The mission itself is in a tolerable state of preservation, though by no means so perfect as San Xavier del Bac. The dome, bell-towers, and adjacent outhouses are considerably defaced by the lapse of time, or more probably by the Vandalism of renegade Americans. A strong adobe corral adjoining the back part of the main edifice, with a massive gateway and with loopholes for purposes of defense, show the insecurity under which the worthy fathers carried on their agricultural pursuits. Valesquez writes in strong terms of the richness and beauty of this part of the valley. I spent some hours making sketches of the ruins, and succeeded, I flatter myself, in getting some tolerably good views, one of which appears on the following page.

Proceeding on our journey, we reached at an early hour in the afternoon the fine old ranch of the Calabasas or "pumpkins." This splendid tract of country belongs, I believe, to Señor Gandara, formerly Governor of Sonora. As an instance of the vicissitudes of life in Sonora, I may mention that we met Señor Gandara just before crossing the Colorado Desert, making his way into California, with a few broken-down retainers, mounted on mules and burrows. All he possessed in the world was a rickety ambulance, his animals, and a few pounds of corn. He was a sad spectacle of a used-up Governor; was old and poor, and had no hope in the future save to die at peace away from the country that gave him birth. The "Calabasas" will never profit him more. An ex-Governor is an outlaw in Sonora. And yet this ranch is one of the finest in the country. It consists of rich bottom lands and rolling hills, extending six leagues up and down the Santa Cruz River by one league in width, embracing excellent pasturage and rich arable lands on both sides. Situated as it is at the junction of the two main roads from Sonora, the Santa Cruz and Magdalena, it might be made a very valuable piece of property in the hands of some enterprising American. A ready market for its productions could always be had at the neighboring silver mines and also at Tucson. At present, however, and until there is military protection in the country, it is utterly worthless, owing to the incursions of the Apaches.

For the past two or three years a stout-hearted frontiersman by the name of Pennington lived at this place, with a family ranging from ten to a dozen daughters, and raised fine crops of corn, besides furnishing the troops at Tucson with a large amount of hay.

"Old Pennington," as he is familiarly called, is one of those strange characters not unfrequently to be met with in the wilds of Arizona. During the whole time of the abandonment of the country by the Americans he occupied with his family a small cabin three miles above the Calabasas, surrounded by roving bands of hostile Indians. He stubbornly refused to leave the country - said he had as much right to it as the infernal Indians, and would live there in spite of all the devils out of the lower regions. His cattle were stolen, his corrals burned down, his fields devastated; yet he bravely stood it out to the last. When hard pressed for food he was compelled to go out in the hills after deer, which he packed in on his back, always at the risk of his life. At times he was several days absent; and I am told his daughters frequently had to stand guard with guns in their hands to keep off the Indians who besieged the premises. One of them, a Mrs. Paige, was on one occasion travelling with her husband, when the Indians attacked the party, killed all the men, beat her on the head with a club, and cast her over a precipice, where they left her for dead. Maimed and bleeding, she crept away during the night, and for sixteen days endured the most dreadful tortures of hunger and thirst, subsisting on roots and berries, and suffering indescribable agony from her wounds. When rescued by a party of whites, she was nothing more than a living skeleton. She now lives with her father, and is an active, hearty woman. Three months ago the family moved down to the neighborhood of Tucson, where I had the pleasure of an introduction to the eccentric "Old Pennington." He is a man of excellent sense, strange as it may seem. Large and tall, with a fine face and athletic frame, he presents as good a specimen of the American frontiersman as I have ever seen. The history of his residence in the midst of the Apaches, with his family of buxom daughters, would fill a volume.

While camped at the Calabasas, some of us slept in the old building, as the nights were rather cool. The escort remained by the bank of the river, which is the best place for pasturage. Calabasas presents something the appearance of a Mexican military post, which I believe it was in former years. The houses are built of stone and adobe, and are still in a good state of preservation, except some of the roofs and a portion of the tower. Major Stein had his headquarters here in 1856-'57. It was occupied for nearly a year by the First Regiment of Dragoons under his command. It was also temporarily occupied by Colonel Ewell, late of the rebel service. A characteristic anecdote of Ewell was related to me during the evening. He wished to procure a supply of water from a spring in one of the neighboring hills, and went out one day with four or five of his men to survey the ground. Having no apprehension of an enemy in such close proximity to his command, he had omitted to take any arms with him, and his men were only provided with axes and spades. About half a mile from the house they were suddenly surprised by a band of Apaches, who commenced shooting at them with their arrows from every bush. The men started to run for the fort, so that they might obtain their arms and make something of a decent fight. "Halt!" shouted Ewell, in stentorian tones, while the arrows fell around him in a perfect shower. "Halt, boys! *let us retreat in good order!*" And, as the story goes, he formed his men in line, and deliberately marched down the hill to an imaginary quickstep, stopping every now and then as the arrows pricked their skins or pierced their clothing to deliver a broadside of imprecations at the cowardly devils who had taken such a dirty advantage of them. It was said of old Ewell that he could swear the scalp off an Apache any time; and one can readily imagine that he did some tall swearing on this occasion.

During the night we were visited by a detachment of the common enemy, evidently on a tour of observation. Next morning their tracks were visible in the road near the river, showing how they had come down and where they halted to inspect the camp, as also their return. Their purpose evidently was to steal our horses; but they must have seen the sentinels and concluded it would not be a safe investment of time or labor. Had the command been less vigilant we would doubtless have made the remainder of our tour on foot, as many a command has already done in this country. Pleasant prospect, is it not? where one stands an even chance of being shot with a rifle-ball or an arrow as he sleeps, and does not know when he wakes up but he may have to cross deserts and mountains on foot before he reaches any point inhabited by white people. But I suppose in war-times, when men are slain every day by thousands, such incidents must appear very tame and commonplace. A few years ago I would have regarded my tour through Arizona as something of achievement. Now I write the details with a humiliating consciousness that they are scarcely worthy of record, except as pictures of every-day life in a country but little known.

As the main object of our journey down in this direction was to ascertain the fate of our American friends who had been waylaid, we posted up notices advising them of our movements in case they should pass along the same road; and determined after some consultation to proceed to Magdalena, Sonora, so as to intercept them in case they had started to return by the way of Guyamas. A few miles beyond Calabasas we encountered a party of Mexicans and Yaqui Indians, on their way up to the placers on the Colorado River, from whom we learned that Mr. Butterworth and his party had passed through Magdalena eight days before. The Mexicans said they met them on the road between Magdalena and Hermosillo, and that they were in an ambulance with a white cover to it, and were travelling "muy racio," with their rifles in their hands. The cover to the ambulance, and some other details, showing the manner in which the Apaches had cut away the leather, identified our friends, and we were satisfied it would be impossible for us to overtake them. It was necessary, however, that we should continue our journey to Magdalena in order to procure a fresh supply of provisions, as we were nearly out, and there was but little prospect of procuring any thing at Santa Cruz.

This day's journey through the valley of Nogales, or the "walnut-trees," was one of the most pleasant of our trip. Every mile we travelled the country improved in beauty and fertility. Grass up to our horses' shoulders covered the valley, and the hills were clothed with luxuriant groves of oak. Much of the country reminded me of the coast range in California.

We stopped awhile at the boundary line to examine the monument erected by Colonel Emory in 1855. Very little of it now remains save an unshapely pile of stones. Wandering bands of Sonoranians, in their hatred of every thing American, had doubtless mutilated it as an expression of national antipathy. These people say they never consented to the sale of any portion of Sonora, and still regard Arizona as legitimately a part of their territory.

I could not help regretting, as I looked beyond the boundary of our territorial possessions, that we had not secured, by purchase or negotiation, a line sufficiently far south to afford us a port on the Gulf of California. Without such a port Arizona will always be difficult of access. Major Fergusson, in his report of a reconnoissance from Port Lobos to Tucson, via Caborea and Arivaca, demonstrates clearly the vast importance of this strip of territory, not only to Arizona but to Mesilla and a large portion of New Mexico. He shows also the urgent desire of the people of the South to secure it, together with Arizona, and the advantages it would give them as a port for their Pacific commerce, in the event of a permanent division of the Union. General Carleton, in transmitting this report to Washington, urges the importance of securing this strip of territory from Mexico before it becomes a possession of France. I do not believe our Government, in the multiplicity of its present labors, is quite aware of the importance of the proposed purchase. It would give to Arizona and its rich mineral regions an easy and direct communication with the Pacific Ocean. It would encourage the settlement of the country by affording facilities for the transportation of mining and agricultural implements and supplies of all kinds, which can now be had only at enormous expense. It would open a route for a railway to the ocean from the valley of the Mesilla. The country is for the most part nearly a level plain, and a very small expenditure of money would make one of the finest wagon-roads in the world from La Libertad to Tucson. The total distance, as measured by Major Fergusson, is 211 miles. It is to be hoped our Government will take this matter into consideration at as early a period as practicable.

AN ARIZONA EPISODE

The evolution of the new woman takes strange phases. A late and unique one is that of her appearance in the character of Dick Turpin. There have been many female stage-robbers in books and stories, but only one in the flesh. Viewed psychologically, the statement of such a woman is curious. Starting with one of the humdrum tragedies that are lived in so many lives, the story of her life is told by herself until it reaches the startling climax with which telegraphic reports have made us familiar. Pearl Hart, the woman who "held up" the Globe stage at Cane Springs canon, Arizona, on May 30th of this year, in company with a male partner, had lived the hard life of the frontier after a disastrous matrimonial experience beginning when she was but sixteen years old. She claims that she was driven to desperation by news of the dangerous illness of her mother. She had no money. She could get none, although she tried in various ways, until, finally, familiar with the exploits of the Western Dick Turpins, she determined to imitate them. She is a small woman, weighing less than a hundred pounds, with features of the most common type. Donning a set of man's clothes and taking the necessary revolver, and securing a male companion, she appeared on the highway. The leveled revolvers quickly brought the coach and its occupants to a standstill. Then, under the cool eye of this bit of a creature, the passengers handed over some four hundred dollars. The attempt to escape, the chase, and the capture that followed—the whole story furnishes an interesting side-light on life in the Southwest.

"When I was but sixteen years old, and while still at boarding school, I fell in love with a man I met in the town in which the school was situated. I was easily impressed. I knew nothing of life. Marriage was to me but a name. It did not take him long to get my consent to an elopement. We ran away one night and were married.

"I was happy for a time, but not for long. My husband began to abuse me, and presently he drove me from him. Then I returned to my mother, in the village of Lindsay, Ontario, where I was born.

"Before long, my husband sent for me, and I went back to him. I loved him, and he promised to do better. I had not been with him two weeks before he began to abuse me again, and after bearing up under his blows as long as I could I left him again. This was just as the World's Fair closed in Chicago, in the fall of 1893. Instead of going home to my mother again, as I should have done, I took the train for Trinidad, Colorado. I was only twenty-two years old. I was good-looking, desperate, discouraged, and ready for anything that might come.

"I do not care to dwell on this period of my life. It is sufficient to say that I went from one city to another until some time later I arrived in Phoenix. I came face to face with my husband on the street one afternoon. I was not then the innocent school-girl he had enticed from home, father, mother, family and friends—far from it. I had been inured to the hardships of the world and knew much of its wickedness. Still, the old infatuation came back. I struggled against it. I knew if I went back to him I should be more unhappy than I was, but I lost the battle. I did go back. We lived together for three years, and I was happy and good, for I dearly loved the man whose name I bore. During the first year of my married life a boy was born to us, and a girl while we were together at Phoenix.

"He was not content. He began to abuse me as of old, and I left him for the third time, vowing never to speak to him again. I sent my children home to my dear old mother and went East, where I supported myself by working as a servant. I heard of my husband occasionally. I tried to forget him, but could not. He was the father of my children and I loved him, in spite of all the abuse he had heaped on me.

"Two years after I had left him the third time, he found out where I was. He came to me and begged me to go back to the West with him, making me all kinds of smooth promises. I went back. I followed him to Tucson. After the money I had saved had been spent, he began beating me, and I lived in hell for months. Finally, he joined McCord's regiment and went to the war. And as for me—why, I went back to Phoenix and got along as best I could.

"I was tired of life. I wanted to die, and tried to kill myself three or four times. I was restrained each time, and finally I got employment cooking for some miners at Mammoth. I lived there for a while, living in a tent pitched on the banks of the Gila river. The work was too hard, and I packed my goods in a wagon and started to go to Globe. I had to return to my old camp because the horses were unable to pull us through. A man named Joe Boot wanted to go to Globe, too, and we made an arrangement with two Mormon boys to freight the whole outfit to Globe for eight dollars. We camped out three miles from Globe, and next day moved in, and I went to work again in a miners' boarding-house. Then one of the big mines shut down and that left me with nothing to do.

"I had saved a little money. One of my brothers found my address and wrote me for some money to help him out of a scrape. I sent him all I had, and was just about to move on to some other town when my husband appeared again. He had been mustered out of his regiment and had followed me to Globe. He was too lazy to work and wanted me to support him. We had another quarrel and parted. I haven't seen him since and I hope I never shall see him again.

"On top of all my other troubles, I got a letter just at this time saying my mother was dying and asking me to come home if I wanted to see her alive again. That letter drove me crazy. No matter what I had been, my mother had been my dearest, truest firend, and I longed to see her again before she died. I had no money. I could get no money. From what I know now, I believe I became temporarily insane.

"Joe Boot, the man who freighted his goods over to Globe with me, told me he had a mining-claim and offered to go out with me and try to dig up enough metal to get a passage home to Canada. We went out to the claim and both worked night and day. It was useless. The claim was no good. I handled pick and shovel like a man, and began wearing man's clothes while I was mining there. I have never worked so hard in my life, and I have had some pretty hard experiences, too.

"When we found there wasn't a sign of color in the claim, I was frantic. I wanted to see my mother. It was the only wish I had. Boot sympathized with me, but he had no money and could not get any. He proposed that we rob the Globe stage. I protested. He said it was the only way to get money. Then I weakened so far as the moral part of it was concerned, but said I was afraid to rob a stage. It seemed a desperate undertaking for a woman of my size. Joe finally said it was easy enough and no one would get hurt. 'A bold front,' he said, 'is all that is necessary to rob any stage.'

" 'Joe', I said, 'if you will promise me that no one will be hurt, I will go with you.'

"He promised, and we made our plans.

"On the afternoon of the robbery we took our horses and rode over the mountains and through the canons, and at last hit the Globe road. We rode along slowly until we came to a bend in the road, which was a most favorable spot for our undertaking. We halted and listened till we heard the stage. Then we went forward on a slow walk, till we saw the stage coming around the bend. We then pulled to one side of the road. Joe drew a 'forty-five,' and said, 'Throw up your hands!' I drew my little 'thirty-eight' and likewise covered the occupants of the stage. Joe said to me, 'Get off your horse.' I did so, while he kept the people covered. He ordered them out of the stage. They were a badly scared outfit. I learned how easily a job of this kind could be done.

"Joe told me to search the passengers for arms. I carefully went through them all. They had no pistols. Joe motioned toward the stage. I advanced and search it, and found the brave passengers had left two of their guns behind them when ordered out of the stage. Really, I can't see why men carry revolvers, because they almost invariably give them up at the very time they were made to be used. They certainly don't want revolvers for playthings. I gave Joe a 'forty-four,' and kept the 'forty-five' for myself. Joe told me to search the passengers for money. I did so, and found on the fellow who was shaking the worst three hundred and ninety dollars. This fellow was trembling so I could hardly get my hand in his pockets. The other fellow, a sort of a dude, with his hair parted in the middle, tried to tell me how much he needed the money, but he yielded thirty-six dollars, a dime and two nickels. Then I searched the remaining passenger, a Chinaman. He was nearer my size and I just scared him to death. His clothes enabled me to go through him quickly. I only got five dollars, however.

"The stage-driver had a few dollars, but after a council of war we decided not to rob him. Then we gave each of the others a charitable contribution of a dollar apiece and ordered them to move on. Joe warning them all not to look back as they valued their lives.

"Joe and I rode slowly up the road for a few miles, planning our future movements. We turned off the well-traveled road to the right. We sought the roughest and most inaccessible region that we could find. We passed at right angles over canons, and repassed those same canons the same day, to cover a trail that we knew would be a hot one before many hours. This undertaking, to throw the officers off the track, was most hazardous, and as I look back upon that wild ride, that effort to escape from the consequences of our bloodless crime, I marvel that we did not lose our lives. As it was, we had many very close escapes. Our horses were likewise in perilous positions several times. It seems to me now that nothing but the excitement of the hour could have carried me through this awful ride, over the perilous trails and the precipitous canons. To-day I cannot tell how we ever got through the ride that day. Many noises in the great mountains and canons led us to believe that our pursuers were at hand, but these turned out to be the workings of our guilty consciences.

"Just at dark that night we came out on the road near Cane Springs. Here Joe led me to take care of the two horses, and went to see if the road ahead was clear. He reported things all right. We then rode toward Riverside, passing that place in the dark about ten o'clock. We continued on for six miles, then crossed the river and camped for the rest of the night and the next day, hobbling our horses as soon as it became dark. We started for the railroad. Our horses were much worn, but in the night we came to a big haystack and got a small feed for each of them, then pushed to within six miles of Mammoth. We were well known there and had to be very careful. We first lay down in the bushes, but we heard wagons pass, and, afterward, men on horseback, which made us very uneasy. We kept quiet until the sounds ceased, then crawled and walked up the side of a big sandstone hill where there were many small caves, or holes, of a circular shape, not much larger than a man's body.

"Upon reaching this spot of safety we found it to be the home of wild or musk hogs, which abound in this locality. These hogs will fight if they have to. However, our peril was so great that we could not hesitate about other chances, and we selected a hole into which we could crawl. Joe started in and I followed. Of course, we had to look out for rattlesnakes, too, which made our entrance very slow. After we had crawled about twenty feet, Joe stopped, saying he could see two shining eyes ahead and was going to take a shot.

"I confess I felt very creepy, but we were between the devil and the deep sea and I listened to hear Joe, from his point ahead of me, tell of his success. The animal was shot and killed, and proved to be a big musk-hog. We soon found the powder-smoke annoying, and as we could not turn around we backed to near the entrance for fresh air. We stayed there all day, and what a long day it was!

"When it got dark we saddled our horses. Joe stole into Mammoth for food and tobacco, and got back without arousing suspicion. After passing Mammoth, we crossed the river and went as far as the school-house, where we hid ourselves and the horses in the bushes at the farther end of a big field. We secured feed for our animals here, and filled a cotton bag with straw to carry. Tired out, we forgot our troubles and slept soundly. At daylight Joe got some food, and we started on; but after going ten miles our horses showed signs of distress, and I realized how much depended on our animals and would have done anything to secure rest and food for them. I remonstrated with my partner about the condition of things, proposing to put our horses in a field and capture others; also to abandon the horses and walk, or to separate for our own safety. His answer was a peremptory No and we pushed on, passing a Mexican squatter's settlement and coming to a wide ditch. My horse jumped across, but Joe's horse fell in, and for a while I thought they would both be drowned. They finally got out. I sat in may saddle perfectly helpless during the struggle.

"This day, which proved to be our last day of freedom, at least for a while, we spent sleeping and cooking. The rain fell in torrents and we were very uncomfortable. At night we again started, and rode until five o'clock in the morning. Just after daylight we came across a mountain lion and gave chase for two miles, but could not get a shot. After this we lay down, but were destined not to sleep long. About three hours after lying down we were awakened by yelling and shooting. We sprang up and grabbed our guns, but found we were looking straight into the mouths of two gaping Winchesters in the hands of the sheriff's posse. Resistance was worse than useless, and we put up hands. At the time of our capture we were within twenty miles of Benson, the railroad station we were making for. Had we reached Benson, I believe we should have escaped.

"We were taken as prisoners first to Benson, thence through Tucson to Casa Grande by rail, and then to Florence. We were kindly treated. The worst thing we suffered was from the curious who came to look at and make fun of us. It would have given me pleasure to meet some of these curious fellows as we met the men in the stage, just to see what they were made of.

"On the 20th, I was transferred to the Tucson jail, as the accommodations here were better adapted to a woman, but I did hate to leave Joe, who had been so considerate of me during all the ups and downs of the wild chase we had been through. His entire trouble was brought on by trying to get money for me to reach mother. We took an oath at parting never to serve out a term in the penitentiary, but rather to find that rest a tired soul seeks. It is, of course, public that I tried to kill myself the day they separated me from Joe at Florence, and to-day I am sorry I didn't succeed.

THE LAST OF THE TERRITORIES

M. G. Cunniff

TEN Congressmen went out to New Mexico and Arizona last fall to find out what the people of these territories thought of being admitted into the Union as one vast state, to be called Arizona, only slightly smaller than Texas. Admission looked probable last year - Oklahoma and Indian Territory as one huge state, Arizona and New Mexico as another. But Arizona hung back. "Rather than join with New Mexico," said its people, "we will gladly remain as we are. Come out here, Easterners, and we'll show you why."

So these ten Congressmen went to New Mexico first. Later Arizona, overjoyed, received them in the lower eastern corner of Cochise County, talked and demonstrated through Pima, Pinal, and Maricopa, converted them in Yavapai, and sent them home through Apache, ready to a man to fight against the merger. And it is a fight. More, it is a national drama. The moves of the statehood campaign have set the United States Senate at loggerheads; they have been marked with crime and ruin in Pennsylvania; they have involved men of many states. But vital as the question is in other parts of the country, it is most vital to those vigorous Americans who are struggling to build commonwealths out of what were but recently stretches of virgin forest and glaring, sunbaked desert. No other question anywhere in the United States is arousing half the red-hot enthusiasm that this is.

I went to the territories just in advance of these Congressmen. I asked every person I met in New Mexico and in Arizona whether he wished joint statehood. New Mexico was lukewarm. Many said, "No." More said, "We want single statehood, but we can't get it. So we will take joint statehood. A half loaf is better than no bread." There was no such wavering in Arizona. Asking that question was like touching a match to a cannon cracker. Men did not merely say, "We don't want joint statehood." They made speeches. They shot forth reasons. They told stories. They made parables. Lawyers overwhelmed me with arguments, doctors analyzed the situation, storekeepers detained me to tell me all about it, conductors hung over rear seats of cars to discuss it; mining men, business men, teachers, editors, Democrats, Republicans, Prohibitionists, were all in the same mood. Sheriff Jim Lowry of Yavapai County, said to me in Prescott, "Sir, I'd like to see Arizona a state. But half a state with New Mexico as the other half? Well, I'd rather see it a territory till I die." This was the gist of what they all said. There are advocates of joint statehood in Arizona. But in an indiscriminate inquiry among all classes of people I could not find one. Behind this remarkable unanimity naturally lies a story.

Last winter's bill to admit Oklahoma and Indian Territory as the new state of Oklahoma, and New Mexico and Arizona as the new state of Arizona passed the House, fell asleep in the Senate, and died with the end of the session. It bound up the fortunes of the proposed Oklahoma with those of the proposed Arizona. Amended in the Senate to admit only the new state of Oklahoma, it never came to acceptance. In the present Congress the new Oklahoma cannot be denied. With its half million of energetic people, its wealth, its bustling towns, its huge crops, its prosperous ranches, its productive mines, it is already a lustier commonwealth than a good half dozen of the states. The point at issue is the admission of New Mexico and Arizona.

Neither territory is the wild waste of cactus-grown desert and bare mountain range, dotted here and there with lawless mining camps and peopled by "bad men," cowboys, and Jack Hamlin gamblers, that fiction has painted. Life in them is no more like that in the

"Arizona Kicker" and in current cheap tales of Western life, than the California mining camps of today are like those that Bret Harte pictured. In the populated districts, it is safer without a "gun" than with one. There is probably less violence in any one day in the territories than on the same day in New York or Chicago. The towns have broad, clean streets and sidewalks, electric lights, good water systems, trolley lines, excellent schools. I would rather send my children to the public schools of Prescott, Ariz., than to most of those in New York - the teaching and the association would be as good, the sanitation better.

Gambling, to be sure, is open. The people in the towns believe that open games of roulette, poker, faro, keno, and craps, such as nightly draw crowds into the saloons, are necessary to lead miners, sheep herders, and other dwellers outside to spend their money in the centers of trade. But all newer communities make the same mistake, and it is far less objectionable to walk down the main street of Albuquerque or of Prescott, within the sound of the rattle of the roulette balls and within sight of the little groups of gamblers, as the doors swing to and fro, than to walk down the Bowery in New York. For these towns keep hidden some kinds of vice that New York obtrudes. The gambling is an evil, but it is as decently managed as open gambling can be. Churches are plentiful and each territory has a fast-growing university and many other educational institutions.

Nor does either territory prove on wider travel to be the sweep of aridness that a through traveler sees much of when crossing the continent by the Santa Fe Railroad on the north or the Southern Pacific on the south. There are indeed miles and aching miles of desert, and the whole lower end of the Rockies flings its huge bulk across the territories. But so vast is their area that besides the deserts and the mountains each contains a greater belt of white pine forest than any state now possesses - a broad band of which is perpetual forest reserve. There are hundreds of miles of broad river valleys now irrigated, or to be irrigated as soon as the government dams now building are completed, 20,000,000 acres in all, that are thrice or four times as fertile under irrigation as the rich valleys of the Connecticut or the Susquehanna. There are mining regions and communities as permanently productive as those of Michigan and Pennsylvania. There are thriving cities like Las Vegas, Albuquerque, Prescott, Phoenix, and Tucson. The territories are more fruitful than they seem.

New Mexico - and Arizona, too, for that matter - believes it ought long ago to have become a state, of itself. As long ago as 1874 a bill granting statehood passed both House and Senate and failed only in conference. Term after term since then, one territorial delegate after another has hammered away for admission. Not long ago Senator Quay of Pennsylvania argued, traded, intrigued, and filibustered for it. The dark story of his reasons will come later in the tale. Senator Beveridge in the last session made the admission of New Mexico, jointly with Arizona, his pet measure, and Mr. B. S. Rodey, the former territorial delegate from New Mexico, devoted his four years of service in the House to pleading for statehood.

Two-thirds of the states had a smaller population than New Mexico when admitted. The territory has an area about equal to New England, New York, and New Jersey combined, and its people are spread all over it. Census enumerators have but thirty days to secure their data and receive but two and one-half cents a name. They simply cannot hunt up all the miners and sheep herders. Many are thus left out. The population is probably somewhat short of 300,000. An Albuquerque newspaper makes an estimate that is doubtless close to correctness - 144,000 people from the states, 127,000 Mexicans, 13,000 Indians. The present valuation of property for tax assessments estimated at about one-fifth the real value is $43,000,000. Taxed at anything like its real worth, this wealth, of course, could easily maintain a state government. And with the further development of the territory, both population and wealth are bound to increase, since the development that present indications promise will be largely agricultural. Today only one acre in 300 is under cultivation.

The territory is now largely dependent on mining, ranching and lumbering. The Colorado Fuel & Iron Company and other interests own iron mines in the north from which 1,000 tons of iron ore a day are shipped to the smelters at Pueblo, Colo. It has anthracite coal and vast beds of bituminous, of which it produces about a million and a half tons a year. There are 2,300 miles of railroad, 1,000 miles of which were built in the last five years. Grant County is said to mine more turquoises than all the rest of the world. New Mexico ships about 200,000 head of cattle a year to be fattened in the Mississippi Valley states. The great Boston wool market is maintained largely through its share of New Mexico's annual output of 25,000,000 pounds. The wool is shipped by way of Galveston, partly to secure cheaper rates, partly because a bag of wool weighs three pounds more when it reaches damp Boston than when it left dry New Mexico. Its gold and silver mines produce about $10,000,000 a year.

I saw at Albuquerque great train loads of logs brought down from the Zuni Mountains to be made into sashes and doors at the mills of the American Lumber Company there, whose thousand employees turn out $1,000,000 worth of manufactured lumber a year. Some of it is shipped by the carload to Galveston for export. Recently several carloads were sent to Glasgow. The waste from the mill runs the electric lighting plant for Albuquerque, whose owners are talking of selling electric power to run pumps for irrigation throughout the valley in which Albuquerque lies. Down in the Mesilla Valley, where the farmers have raised huge crops of alfalfa, grain, and fruits in good years, the Government is pushing forward the Elephant Butte Dam project to impound the water that runs to waste in the spring; and, when that is completed, agriculture will be as certain an enterprise there as an ideal climate for crops can make it. Already settlers from Texas are flocking into the valley to take up the small allotments permitted under the provisions of the irrigation project; for one acre of irrigated land in that climate is as productive as four in a land of rainfall. Similar irrigation projects are under way in other parts of the territory - the Hondo, the La Plata, and the Las Vegas projects - and many acres are irrigated by private enterprise. The Estancia Valley already has a reputation for its fruits, and the orchards of Colfax are a delight to the eye. When the irrigation works now being pushed are completed, New Mexico's agricultural output will be considerable. Water is the prime necessity, and there is plenty of water if it can only be controlled, or pumped up. In places it is but a little way under the ground. Deming, near the Mexican line, is a little paradise of green fields and whirling windmills. For years one of its leading products was water, which was sent by the railroad to El Paso, Texas, and sold there.

A Large part of the territory is not divided into small holdings, as in most of the states, but is covered by vast land grants running back to the Spanish occupation - princely domains, in many cases owned by people outside the territory and rented largely to Mexican ranchers and farmers. Because of these huge grants New Mexico is - in spite of its wide stretches of public domain - less open to homesteading than one might suppose, for practically all the good land not owned by small farmers is embraced in them.

But after all the chief problem lies in the people

of the territory. Albuquerque gives a fair impression of town life in the northern part. It is the largest city, with perhaps a population of 10,000. Just outside its limits is Old Town, the historic Albuquerque of Spanish and Mexican tradition. Walk on a moonlight night through its unlighted streets flanked by squat lines of adobe dwellings, to the little plaza fronted by the church built by mission *padres*, and, standing there, you will be aware of nothing to make you believe the time later than the seventeenth century. A dark figure will move silently along in the dust of the street, appearing and disappearing as it crosses the checkerboards of moonlight and black shadow, and suddenly slip noiselessly through the apparently blank side of a dwelling. You may hear a guitar or a mandolin. The scene is all Spanish or all Mexican, as you will. It is not American - till you hear the buzz of a trolley car, and you hurry out of this fixed survival of a dead century to be whirled a mile or so back into as busy a little city as can be found in the West. This is the modern Albuquerque, with brilliantly lighted streets, factories, mills, and banks, a school in every ward, and a Commercial Club that would not be out of place in New York, built up by people of education and enterprise. What strikes an observer is that Old Town with its 2,000 or more Mexicans sits there cheek by jowl with the modern Albuquerque with its 10,000 or more Americans with a fair proportion of Mexicans among them. Elsewhere the proportion of Mexicans is larger. Santa Fe is more Mexican than Albuquerque - a town older by three-quarters of a century than Jamestown or Plymouth. For all its modern capitol it has a Mexican air. Outside of the towns in the northern part of the territory the proportion of Mexicans is more than half. Some counties are almost wholly Mexican. All told, between two-fifths and one-half the people are Mexicans.

Some are descendants of aristocratic Spanish families still conducting in almost feudal fashion vast sheep ranges on lands granted to their ancestors by the Spanish crown. Or they are progressive business men differing no more from their American associates than the casual Germans or Jews or Frenchmen with whom they daily do business. They are Spaniards or Mexicans, but Americanized. Senator Beveridge on a flying trip of investigation through the territories asked Mr. Isidoro Armijo, the probate clerk of Donna Ana County, if he were not a Mexican. "No," was the reply. "But your parents were Mexican?" asked the Senator. "Yes," said Mr. Armijo, "and yours were German, but that doesn't make you Dutch."

Mr. Solomon Luna, the richest sheepman of the territory, president of the Commercial Bank of Albuquerque, is another who considers himself an American. His home is in a hacienda at Los Lunas, and he feeds his 60,000 sheep over practically the whole of Valencia County. He does not own all the land - much of it is still public domain - but he owns the water courses, which means that he monopolizes the resources of the region through which they run. He has 5,000 acres of irrigated land under cultivation. He maintains hundreds of Mexican employees. The territorial Governor, Miguel Otero, who has just been replaced by the President's new appointee, Mr. A. Haggerman of Roswell, is another prominent citizen who is a descendant of an old Spanish family of influence in the territory since the days of the Spanish occupation.

But with all the sprinkling of men like these, there are tens of thousands of ordinary Mexicans, alien in blood, language, tradition, political consciousness, and temper of mind to the Americans who are building up the territory. And they vote.

Intermarriage of Americans and Mexicans is not uncommon. The little Mexicans go to school with the little Americans. Practically all the Mexicans are devout Roman Catholics, and the Church is very strong in the territory. Naturally a large proportion of the Mexican children go to the church schools. The territorial Legislature always contains a number of Mexicans. In some counties the Mexicans dominate. Mr. Armijo, who made the retort to Senator Beveridge, keeps some of the records of Donna Ana in Spanish, and I have been told that records are so kept in other counties. Interpreters are required in the courts to interpret Mexican testimony to the American half of the jury and American testimony to the Mexican half. A brief visit to a court in Albuquerque brought me upon the startling scene of a lawyer addressing a jury with the assistance of an interpreter. The lawyer would pause intermittenly, whereupon the interpreter would translate his words and even mimic his gestures. Naturally, interpreters are required in jury rooms to make the reasoning of the alien jurymen plain to one another, in order that a verdict may be reached. The territory then is very much Mexicanized. Political bosses wield their power because they can "swing the Mexican vote."

"Why," said an Albuquerque man to me jocosely, "they say that over in Donna Ana County they vote the sheep."

When I pressed for the amount of truth behind the joke he said: "They vote the Mexican herders and that's not much different from voting the sheep."

Two brothers Hubbell were the bosses of Bernalillo County. Indeed one of them, Mr. Frank Hubbell, was the Republican boss of the territory until the recent overturn which brought Mr. W. H. Andrews into that position. One brother was sheriff of the county, the other was treasurer and collector. They are half Mexican. They know how to handle the Mexican voters. They appointed one Eslavio Vijil county superintendent of schools. A common report was that he could neither read nor write. Though this was not true, he had as much fitness for the place as a Chicago ward heeler. Jurymen were drawn not by lot, but by selection by an officer of the court who chose them from the jury list. It was said that a litigant, by seeing one of the Hubbells, could practically pick his own jury, or pick at least a venal one. It was only after the exposure of the alleged wrong doings that the lot system of selection was established last fall. Last summer Governor Otero removed the Hubbells and Vijil from office.

Nor are other examples of Mexican preeminence in politics lacking. Mr. Pedro Perea of Bernalillo was territorial delegate to the Fifty-sixth Congress. In several of the counties the school superintendents are Mexicans. Mr. Elfego Baca wanted to be district attorney of Socorro County. He fought the administration until they capitulated, and his reward was the district attorneyship of both Socorro and Sierra counties - the salary of one office was not large enough to satisfy him. He is now boss of both counties. Mr. Eugenio Romero is boss of San Miguel County. And so it goes.

Mr. Rodey, who speaks well of the Mexicans, said to me, "They do not go into corrupt deals except under the leadership and with the encouragement of Americans from the states." Now see what happened on this head. Mr. W. H. Andrews, the now notorious "Bull" Andrews, came out to Albuquerque to see what he could do with some properties in which he and certain other Pennsylvania politicians were interested. He came from Meadville, Penn. For years he had been the political henchman of Senator Quay in the devious machinations that such service called for in western Pennsylvania and about the capitol at Harrisburg. The New Mexico enterprises of Mr. Andrews and his friends were carried on under the corporation names of the Pennsylvania Development Company and the New Mexico Fuel & Iron Company. While in Albuquerque, Mr. Andrews lived at a

hotel. It was understood in the town that he still
kept a Pennsylvania residence - in Pittsburg. But
sumptuous offices were maintained in Albuquerque.
The company had coal land and timber land. It set to
work building railroads, partly to open them up, and
partly as a good speculation in itself. The Santa Fe
Central was built from Santa Fe to Torrance on the
Rock Island Railroad, and the Albuquerque Eastern was
then set going from Albuquerque to Moriarty on the
other line. A branch line was projected to strike the
Hagan coal fields of the subsidiary company, the New
Mexico Fuel & Iron Company. Other subsidiary companies were organized to build other lines. The Quay
politicians, with Mr. W. H. Andrews at the head, were
the most active promoters in the territory. "Bull"
Andrews early let it be known that he wanted to be
Senator from the new state of New Mexico, and his
friend and patron Senator Quay was willing to help his
ambition. Quay fought for statehood tooth and nail in
the Senate, and, threatening to "hold up" all other
legislation until New Mexico was granted statehood,
succeeded in delaying the Senate's business throughout
nearly all of one session.

Why was Andrews's need to be Senator so urgent? I
asked for him at his office in Albuquerque in October.
I was told that he was East on business. He was.
Within a fortnight the cashier of the Enterprise Bank
of Pittsburg committed suicide, leaving a note behind
saying that Andrews had worked both his ruin and the
bank's. The bank was wrecked, swamped by the loans it
had made to the Pennsylvania Development Company and
Mr. Andrews; and it was charged that the loans had
been made through the criminal complicity of the bank
officers with Andrews. The hope of Quay and of Andrews
had been that New Mexico would be made a state and
Andrews its first Senator. How this would serve the
Pennsylvania Development Company Mr. Andrews, who is
credited with knowing the devices of commercialism in

politics better than most men, knows best, but it is asserted that he hoped to get the new state of New Mexico to guarantee his railroad bonds.

Mr. B. S. Rodey had served several terms as territorial delegate to Congress, and had worked as no other New Mexican has worked for statehood. He is now the most ardent advocate of joint statehood in the country, a lawyer, enthusiastic, argumentative, popular. Last year he came up for re-election. Mr. Andrews was one of his most vociferous supporters. Mr. Rodey was so confident of the Republican nomination that he scarcely made a campaign. His friend, Mr. Andrews, in part attended to that. The delegates from the counties were Rodey delegates. When the convention met, to the vast astonishment of most people in the territory, Mr. Andrews and not Mr. Rodey was nominated - and later elected. The methods by which the delegates were converted almost over night are said in New Mexico to have been a new kind of politics imported from Pennsylvania. Almost over night Mr. Andrews replaced Mr. Rodey as territorial delegate, and replaced Mr. Frank Hubbell as Republican boss of New Mexico. Even a friend and a well-wisher of the territory must think that New Mexico is not in a position to saddle its problems on Arizona. No better type of American exists in the West than the average American dweller in New Mexico, but the possible effects of Pennsylvania political methods on Mexican voters do not look attractive in the light of the easy success of such a man as "Bull" Andrews.

Now it is just this phase of the situation in New Mexico that makes a large part of Arizona's case. There are not more than 150,000 people in Arizona, more than 25,000 of whom are Indians on reservations, who of course do not count. But Arizona is not a half Mexican community. The 125,000 people there are vigorous, enterprising Americans. It is asserted that there is a larger proportion of college graduates among them

than in any other population of similar size in the
country - engineers, lawyers, doctors, business men,
farmers. The proportion of college men I met there
makes me easily believe it. I visited schools, and
found well paid college and normal school graduates
teaching bright children under sanitary conditions
and according to modern methods. The schools in
Prescott and in Phoenix are as good as those in Boston. The men - and the women, too - take pride in
their towns, take pride in their territory. Arizona
is as different from New Mexico as Texas is. Its
dwellers are no better than the somewhat larger number of Americans in New Mexico, but they do not share
their common life with an alien people, and they do
not want to. But in a state made of the two territories, the 300,000 people of the New Mexico end would
outvote the 125,000 people of the Arizona end, and
the new state would naturally assume the New Mexico
tone.

"Would the people of Massachusetts," asked a lawyer in Phoenix, "be willing to have Congress peremptorily merge the state with New York? Well, that's
our situation."

The new state of Oklahoma will probably be Democratic. Is Senator Beveridge, the leader of the joint
statehood movement, trying to drag Arizona in as a
make-weight for New Mexico in order to create a
Republican state to balance it? If Congress will not
admit the territories separately, and it is not to be
expected that four United States Senatorships will be
handed to less than half a million people, the people
of Arizona are content to wait until they have built
a state. They beg that New Mexico, too, be allowed
to stand on its own merits, to come in or to stay out
according to its own achievements.

If it were true that Arizona is not likely within
a reasonable time to attain statehood stature, Congress might well say, "We want to end territorial
government within our boundaries. If you are not able

to stand alone with the other commonwealths, you and New Mexico together surely can. Your 125,000 people together with their 155,000 brothers in New Mexico will learn in time how to manage the Mexican element, and, in the great new state, American ideas and American progressiveness are bound to prevail." But Arizona is in no such position. Its people maintain that the territory is fit for statehood now - as in everything else than population it is - and the very spirit of their daily work is the indomitable ambition to build a vigorous commonwealth.

In 1870 there were but 172 farms in the territory, covering but 22,000 acres. By 1890 there were 1,400 with 1,300,000 acres. In 1900 there were nearly 6,000 with nearly 2,000,000 acres and worth nearly $30,000,000. This land, practically all under irrigation, produced a return averaging more than $60 an acre. This advance tells the story of plucky business men and farmers who met the irrigation problem and solved it with their own brains and their own capital.

Now that the Government has taken hold of it, and the Colorado River, the Salt, and the Gila are to be robbed of their floods to fill irrigation ditches as soon as the dams are completed at Rincon and Yuma, new miles of rich alfalfa fields and fruitful orchards will widen Arizona's strips of green carpet. Oranges ripen in the Salt River Valley earlier than anywhere else in the United States, and they bring a higher price than any others. Dates are now being grown successfully there. There is no better climate for melons, fruits, grains, and alfalfa than southern Arizona; there is no agricultural enterprise more alluring than intensive farming where there is no possibility of crop failures. People are only too ready to flock in wherever water can be had, and these farmers who come in are men of the same type that have made the commonwealth of Oklahoma. More will come in, when the Yuma and the Tonto dams are completed. There are 10,000,000 acres of land in the territory susceptible of irrigation and only 1,000,000 acres have thus far been reclaimed.

Besides the farms, Arizona has leagues of grazing land, on which I saw sleek herds of fattening cattle, and its forests are even greater in extent than those of New Mexico. Lumber is shipped from Flagstaff to all parts of the country. About 200,000,000 feet of lumber is cut every year, mostly in the northern part of the territory. Much of it is shipped in manufactured form. About $3,000,000 worth of sheep, cattle, and horses are sold from the ranges annually. But the chief asset of the territory is her wealth of minerals. Arizona is now the leading copper producing center of the world, and its output of gold and silver is very considerable. Its total mining output amounts to more than $40,000,000 a year. Mines like the United Verde and the Copper Queen support prosperous towns like Bisbee, Globe, and Jerome. There are nearly 2,000 patented mines, and all mining experts agree that the 30,000,000 acres of Arizona's mineral belt have thus far been merely scratched.

Twenty-four states have been admitted to the Union with a smaller population than Arizona now has, and twenty-seven with a smaller amount of taxable property. If the standard for admission has been raised with advancing years, the people of the territory are not faint-hearted about their ability to attain any standard Congress may set. They are willing to stay out until they attain it. The few advocates of joint statehood in the territory - I received a letter after leaving the territory from a small joint statehood association in Pima County - assert that the corporations which own the great mines and the railroads in Arizona are behind the anti-joint statehood movement. It is true that they are opposed to the merger of the territory with New Mexico, because they do not wish to run the danger of being taxed as the proposed state, managed by the New Mexican end, might tax them. But to maintain that the corporations are responsible for so nearly unanimous a feeling as seems to exist in Arizona is futile. They could not do it. They might reach some of the people; they could not fool practically all. The explanation is simpler. Americans buildinga commonwealth take a jealous pride in its integrity. All Arizona asks is a square deal. The Foraker amendment to the statehood bill of last year provided that the question of admission be submitted to popular vote in both territories, each voting separately. This would be a fair method of settling the difficulty.

VETO ON ARIZONA STATEHOOD

William Howard Taft

To the House of Representatives:

I return herewith, without my approval, House joint resolution No. 14, "To admit the Territories of New Mexico and Arizona as States into the Union on an equal footing with the original States."

Congress, by an enabling act approved June 20, 1910, provided for the calling of a constitutional convention in each of these Territories, the submission of the constitution proposed by the convention to the electors of the Territory, the approval of the constitution by the President and Congress, the proclamation of the fact by the President, and the election of State officers. Both in Arizona and New Mexico conventions have been held, constitutions adopted and ratified by the people and submitted to the President and Congress. I have approved the constitution of New Mexico, and so did the House of Representatives of the Sixty-first Congress. The Senate, however, failed to take action upon it. I have not approved the Arizona constitution, nor have the two Houses of Congress, except as they have done so by the joint resolution under consideration. The resolution admits both Territories to statehood with their constitutions, on condition that at the time of the election of State officers New Mexico shall submit to its electors an amendment to its new constitution altering and modifying its provision for future amendments, and on the further condition that Arizona shall submit to its electors, at the time of the election of its State officers, a proposed amendment to its constitution by which judicial officers shall be excepted from the section permitting a recall of all elective officers.

If I sign this joint resolution, I do not see how I can escape responsibility for the judicial recall of the Arizona constitution. The joint resolution admits Arizona with the judicial recall, but requires the submission of the question of its wisdom to the voters. In other words, the resolution approves the admission of Arizona with the judicial recall, unless the voters themselves repudiate it. Under the Arizona constitution all elective officers, and this includes county and State judges, six months after their election are subject to the recall. It is initiated by a petition signed by electors equal to 25 per cent of the total number of votes cast for all the candidates for the officer at the previous general election. Within five days after the petition is filed the officer may resign. Whether he does or not, an election ensues in which his name, if he does not resign, is placed on the ballot with that of all other candidates. The petitioners may print on the official ballot 200 words showing their reasons for recalling the officer, and he is permitted to make defense in the same place in 200 words. If the incumbent receives the highest number of the votes, he continues in his office; if not, he is removed from office and is succeeded by the candidate who does receive the highest number.

This provision of the Arizona constitution, in its application to county and State judges, seems to me so pernicious in its effect, so destructive of independence in the judiciary, so likely to subject the rights of the individual to the possible tyranny of a popular majority, and, therefore, to be so injurious to the cause of free government, that I must disapprove a constitution containing it. I am not now engaged in performing the office given me in the enabling act already referred to, approved June 20, 1910, which was that of approving the constitutions ratified by the peoples of the Territories. It may be argued from the text of that act that in giving or withholding the approval under the act my only duty is to examine the proposed constitution, and if I find nothing in it inconsistent with the Federal Constitution, the principles of the Declaration of Independence, or the enabling act, to register my approval. But now I am discharging my constitutional function in respect to the enactment of laws, and my discretion is equal to that of the Houses of Congress. I must therefore withhold my approval from this resolution if in fact I do not approve it as a matter of governmental policy. Of course, a mere difference of opinion as to the wisdom of details in a State constitution ought not to lead me to set up my opinion against that of the people of the Territory. It is to be their government, and while the power of Congress to withhold or grant statehood is absolute, the people about to constitute a State should generally know better the kind of government and constitution suited to their needs than Congress or the Executive. But when such a constitution contains something so destructive of free government as the judicial recall, it should be disapproved.

A government is for the benefit of all the people. We believe that this benefit is best accomplished by popular government, because in the long run each class of individuals is apt to secure better provision for themselves through their own voice in government than through the altruistic interest of others, however intelligent or philanthropic. The wisdom of ages has taught that no government can exist except in accordance with laws and unless the people under it either obey the laws voluntarily or are made to obey them. In a popular government the laws are made by the people—not by all the people—but by those supposed and declared to be competent for the purpose, as males over 21 years of age, and not by all of these—but by a majority of them only. Now, as the government is for all the people, and is not solely for a majority of them, the majority in exercising control either directly or through its agents is bound to exercise the power for the benefit of the minority as well as the majority. But all have recognized that the majority of a people, unrestrained by law, when aroused and without the sobering effect of deliberation and discussion, may do injustice to the minority or to the individual when the selfish interest of the majority prompts. Hence arises the necessity for a constitution by which the will of the majority shall be permitted to guide the course of the government only under controlling checks that experience has shown to be necessary to secure for the minority its share of the benefit to the whole people that a popular government is established to bestow. A popular government is not a government of a majority, by a majority, for a majority of the people. It is a government of the whole people by a majority of the whole people under such rules and checks as will secure a wise, just, and beneficent government for all the people. It is said you can always trust the people to do justice. If that means all the people and they all agree, you can. But ordinarily they do not all agree, and the maxim is interpreted to mean that you can always trust a majority of the people. This is not invariably true; and every limitation imposed by the people upon the power of the majority in their constitutions is an admission that it is not always true. No honest, clear-headed man, however great a lover of popular government, can deny that the unbridled expression of the majority of a community converted hastily into law or action would sometimes make a government tyrannical and cruel. Constitutions are checks upon the hasty action of the majority. They are the self-imposed restraints of a whole people upon a majority of them to secure sober action and a respect for the rights of the minority, and of the individual in his relation to other individuals, and in his relation to the whole people in their character as a state or government.

The Constitution distributes the functions of government into three branches—the legislative, to make the laws; the executive, to execute them; and the judicial, to decide in cases arising before it the rights of the individual as between him and others and as between his and the Government. This division of government into three separate branches has always been regarded as a great security for the maintenance of free institutions, and the security is only firm and assured when the judicial branch is independent and impartial. The executive and legislative branches are representative of the majority of the people which elected them in guiding the course of the Government within the limits of the Constitution. They must act for the whole people, of course; but they may properly follow, and usually ought to follow, the views of the majority which elected them in respect to the governmental policy best adapted to secure the welfare of the whole people. But the judicial branch of the Government is not representative of a majority of the people in any such sense, even if the mode of selecting judges is by popular election. In a proper sense, judges are servants of the people; that is, they are doing work which must be done for the Government and in the interest of all the people, but it is not work in the doing of which they are to follow the will of the majority except as that is embodied in statutes lawfully enacted according to constitutional limitations. They are not popular representatives. On the contrary, to fill their office properly they must be independent. They must decide every question which comes before them according to law and justice. If this question is between individuals, they will follow the statute, or the unwritten law if no statute applies, and they take the unwritten law growing out of tradition and custom from previous judicial decisions. If a statute or ordinance affecting a cause before them is not lawfully enacted, because it violates the constitution adopted by the people, then they must ignore the statute and decide the question as if the statute had never been passed. This power is a judicial power imposed by the people on the judges by the written constitution. In early days some argued that the obligations of the Constitution operated directly on the conscience of the legislature, and only in that manner, and that it was to be conclusively presumed that whatever was done by the legislature was constitutional. But such a view did not obtain with our hard-headed, courageous, and far-sighted statesmen and judges, and it was soon settled that it was the duty of judges in cases properly arising before them to apply the law and so to declare what was the law, and that if what purported to be statutory law was at variance with the fundamental law, i.e., the Constitution, the seeming statute was not law at all, was not binding on the courts, the individuals, or any branch of the Government, and that it was the duty of the judges so to decide. This power conferred on the judiciary in our form of government is unique in the history of governments, and its operation has attracted and deserved the admiration and commendation of the world. It gives to our judiciary a position higher, stronger, and more responsible than that of the judiciary of any other country, and more effectively secures adherence to the fundamental will of the people.

What I have said has been to little purpose if it has not shown that judges to fulfill their functions properly in our popular Government must be more independent than in any other form of government, and that need of independence is greatest where the individual is one litigant and the State, guided by the successful and governing majority, is the other. In order to maintain the rights of the minority and the individual and to preserve our constitutional balance, we must have judges with courage to decide against the majority when justice and law require.

By the recall in the Arizona constitution it is proposed to give to the majority power to remove arbitrarily, and without delay, any judge who may have the courage to render an unpopular decision. By the recall it is proposed to enable a minority of 25 per cent of the voters of the district or State, for no prescribed cause, after the judge has been in office six months, to submit the question of his retention in office to the electorate. The petitioning minority must say on the ballot what they can against him in 200 words, and he must defend as best he can in the same space. Other candidates are permitted to present themselves and have their names printed on the ballot, so that the recall is not based solely on the record or the acts of the judge, but also on the question whether some other and more popular candidate has been found to unseat him. Could there be a system more ingeniously devised to subject judges to momentary gusts of popular passion than this? We can not be blind to the fact that often an intelligent and respectable electorate may be so roused upon an issue that it will visit with condemnation the decision of a just judge, though exactly in accord with the law governing the case, merely because it affects unfavorably their contest. Controversies over elections, labor troubles, racial or religious issues, issues as to the construction or constitutionality of liquor laws, criminal trials of popular or unpopular defendants, the removal of county seats, suits by individuals to maintain their constitutional rights in obstruction of some popular improvement—these and many other cases could be cited in which a majority of a district electorate would be tempted by hasty anger to recall a conscientious judge if the opportunity were open all the time. No period of delay is interposed for the abatement of popular feeling. The recall is devised to encourage quick action and to lead the people to strike while the iron is hot. The judge is treated as the instrument and servant of a majority of the people and subject to their momentary will, not after a long term in which his qualities as a judge and his character as a man have been subjected to a test of all the varieties of judicial work and duty so as to furnish a proper means of measuring his fitness for continuance in another term. On the instant of an unpopular ruling, while the spirit of protest has not had time to cool, and even while an appeal may be pending from his ruling, in which he may be sustained, he is to be haled before the electorate as a tribunal, with no judicial hearing, evidence, or defense, and thrown out of office and disgraced for life because he has failed, in a single decision, it may be, to satisfy the popular demand. Think of the opportunity such a system would give to unscrupulous political bosses in control, as they have been in control not only of conventions but elections! Think of the enormous power for evil given to the sensational, muckraking portion of the press in rousing prejudice against a just judge by false charges and insinuations, the effect of which in the short period of an election by recall it would be impossible for him to meet and offset! Supporters of such a system seem to think that it will work only in the interest of the poor, the humble, the weak and the oppressed; that it will strike down only the judge who is supposed to favor corporations and be affected by the corrupting influence of the rich. Nothing could be further from the ultimate result. The motive it would offer to unscrupulous combinations to seek to control politics in order to control the judges is clear. Those would profit by the recall who have the best opportunity of rousing the majority of the people to action on a sudden impulse. Are they likely to be the wisest or the best people in a community? Do they not include those who have money enough to employ the firebrands and slanderers in a community and the stirrers-up of social hate? Would not self-respecting men well hesitate to accept judicial office with such a sword of Damocles hanging over them? What kind of judgments might those on the unpopular side expect from courts whose judges must make their decisions under such legalized terrorism? The character of the judges would deteriorate to that of trimmers and timeservers, and independent judicial action would be a thing of the past. As the possibilities of such a system pass in review, is it too much to characterize it as one which will destroy the judiciary, its standing, and its usefulness?

The argument has been made to justify the judicial recall that it is only carrying out the principle of the election of the judges by the people. The appointment by the executive is by the representative of the majority, and so far as future bias is concerned there is no great difference between the appointment and the election of judges. The independence of the judiciary is secured rathe; by a fixed term and fixed and irreducible salary. It is true that when the term of judges is for a limited number of years and reelection is necessary, it has been thought and charged sometimes that shortly before election in cases in which popular interest is excited, judges have leaned in their decisions toward the popular side.

As already pointed out, however, in the election of judges for a long and fixed term of years, the fear of popular prejudice as a motive for unjust decisions is minimized by the tenure on the one hand, while the opportunity which the people have calmly to consider the work of a judge of a full term of years in deciding as to his reelection generally insures from them a fair and reasonable consideration of his qualities as a judge. While, therefore, there have been elected judges who have bowed before unjust popular prejudice, or who have yielded to the power of political bosses in their decisions, I am convinced that these are exceptional, and that, on the whole, elected judges have made a great American judiciary. But the success of an elective judiciary certainly furnishes no reason for so changing the system as to take away the very safeguards which have made it successful.

Attempt is made to defend the principle of judicial recall by reference to States in which judges are said to have shown themselves to be under corrupt corporate influence and in which it is claimed that nothing but a desperate remedy will suffice. If the political control in such States is sufficiently wrested from corrupting corporations to permit the enactment of a radical constitutional amendment like that of judicial recall, it would seem possible to make provision in its stead for an effective remedy by impeachment in which the cumbrous features of the present remedy might by avoided, but the opportunity for judicial hearing and defense before an impartial tribunal might be retained. Real reforms are not to be effected by patent short cuts or by abolishing those requirements which the experience of ages has shown to be essential in dealing justly with everyone. Such innovations are certain in the long run to plague the inventor or first user and will come readily to the hand of the enemies and corrupters of society after the passing of the just popular indignation that prompted their adoption.

Again, judicial recall is advocated on the ground that it will bring the judges more into sympathy with the popular will and the progress of ideas among the people. It is said that now judges are out of touch with the movement toward a wider democracy and a greater control of governmental agencies in the interest and for the benefit of the people. The righteous and just course for a judge to pursue is ordinarily fixed by statute or clear principles of law, and the cases in which his judment may be affected by his political, economic, or social views are infrequent. But even in such cases judges are not removed from the people's influence. Surround the judiciary with all the safeguards possible, create judges by appointment, make their tenure for life, forbid diminution of salary during their term, and still it is impossible to prevent the influence of popular opinion from coloring judgments in the long run. Judges are men, intelligent, sympathetic men, patriotic men, and in those fields of the law in which the personal equation unavoidably plays a part, there will be found a response to sober popular opinion as it changes to meet the exigency of social, political, and economic changes. Indeed, this should be so. Individual instances of a hidebound and retrograde conservatism on the part of courts in decisions which turn on the individual economic or sociological views of the judges may be pointed out; but they are not many, and do not call for radical action. In treating of courts we are dealing with a human machine, liable, like all the inventions of man, to err, but we are dealing with a human institution that likens itself to a divine institution, because it seeks and preserves justice. It has been the corner stone of our gloriously free Government, in which the rights of the individual and of the minority have been preserved, while governmental action of the majority has lost nothing of beneficent progress, efficacy, and directness. This balance was planned in the Constitution by its framers, and has been maintained by our independent judiciary.

Precedents are cited from State constitutions said to be equivalent to a popular recall. In some, judges are removable by a vote of both houses of the legislature. This is a mere adoption of the English address of Parliament of the Crown for the removal of judges. It is similar to impeachment, in that a form of hearing is always granted. Such a provision forms no precedent for a popular recall without adequate hearing and defense, and with new candidates to contest the election.

It is said the recall will be rarely used. If so, it will be rarely needed. Then why adopt a system so full of danger? But it is a mistake to suppose that such a powerful lever for influencing judicial decisions and such an opportunity for vengeance because of adverse ones will be allowed to remain unused.

But it is said that the people of Arizona are to become an independent State when created, and even if we strike out judicial recall now, they can reincoporate it in their constitution after statehood.

To this I would answer that in dealing with the courts, which are the corner stone of good government, and in which not only the voters, but the nonvoters and nonresidents, have a deep interest as a security for their rights of life, liberty, and property, no matter what the future action of the State may be, it is necessary for the authority which is primarily responsible for its creation to assert in no doubtful tones the necessity for an independent and untrammeled judiciary.

Wm. H. Taft.

The White House, *August 15, 1911.*

DOCUMENTS

ARIZONA AND THE RECALL OF THE JUDICIARY

Theodore Roosevelt

New Mexico and Arizona are entitled to be admitted as States. In New Mexico's case there is no objection anywhere, and not a valid reason can be assigned for the failure to have admitted her several months ago. Without any regard to Arizona, New Mexico should be admitted at once.

But Arizona also should clearly, and as a matter of right and duty, at once be admitted to Statehood. The only objection of consequence to admitting her is that her Constitution provides for the recall of judges. Outside of this provision no serious objection has been made to her Constitution, and personally, after considerable study of the document, I have come to the conclusion that it is an unusually good Constitution; that while, of course, it contains certain provisions as to which there will be considerable dissent, yet that, as a whole, it is a Constitution well above the average, a Constitution which in many vital respects it would be an admirable thing to have imitated in New York and elsewhere in the East. The whole question, therefore, narrows down to the point as to whether it is legitimate to reject Arizona's plea because she has done what Oregon has done, what California has announced she will do - that is, because Arizona desires, when she is a State, to have the same privilege which these two States possess and exercise. Moreover, it must be remembered that, if the people of Arizona desire to exercise the right of recall of the judges, their desire can be made effective immediately after their admission to Statehood; even though, in order to get in, they consent to alter the provision in their Constitution as proposed. It seems to me that the mere statement of these facts is sufficient to show that, on the ground alleged, there is no excuse for failure to admit Arizona to Statehood.

Personally, I do not think that under normal circumstances it is advisable to have the principle of the popular recall applied to the judiciary. I much prefer the Massachusetts system, under which a judge can be removed by vote of the two branches of the legislative body without trial and on simple assignment of reasons. But the fact that I and other people feel a preference for one system has nothing whatever to do with Arizona's right to adopt another system, and it is an absurdity to say that the adoption of the other system, that of the recall, would make the Arizona government not a republican form of government. The difference between a judicial system under which judges are appointed for life and are removable only after impeachment, and a system under which judges are elected for short terms, is infinitely greater than the difference between the latter system - that is, a short-term elective judiciary without a recall - and the proposed Arizona system of a short-term elective judiciary with a recall. The assertion that both the first two are compatible with the existence of a republican form of government, and that the latter is not, is really hardly worth serious discussion. Massachusetts has one system for her judiciary, New York another, Ohio a third; and in vital and essential matters they differ more among themselves than at least one of them differs from that proposed for Arizona. It would be quite improper for Massachusetts to impose its system upon Ohio, or Ohio its system upon Massachusetts, or for Texas to impose its system upon New York, or New York its system upon Texas; and it is just as improper for all four to impose upon Arizona the system of any one of them, or to refuse to permit Arizona to have the system which Arizona desires.

Moreover, in all these matters it is well to remember that the thing, and not the name, is essential.

If in any given State the system of an elective or an appointive judiciary without a recall has proved in actual practice to work badly (as it certainly proved to work badly in California), then practical reformers who are working for the betterment of popular conditions are quite right in trying to substitute for it some other system. The all-important thing is the spirit in which the system is administered. If in any State the adoption of the recall was found to mean the subjection of the judge to the whim of the mob, then it would become the imperative duty of every good citizen, without regard to previous prejudices, to work for the alteration of the system. If, on the other hand, in any State the judiciary yields to improper influence on the part of special interests, or if the judges even, although honest men, show themselves so narrowminded and so utterly out of sympathy with the industrial and social needs brought about by changed conditions that they seek to fetter the movement for progress and betterment, then the people are not to be excused if, in a servile spirit, they submit to such domination, and fail to take any measures necessary to secure their right to go forward along the path of economic and social justice and fair dealing. If our people are really fit for self-government, then they will insist upon governing themselves. In all matters affecting the Nation as a whole this power of self-government should reside in the majority of the Nation as a whole; and upon this doctrine no one has insisted more strongly than I have insisted, for in such case "popular rights" becomes a meaningless phrase save as it is translated into National rights. But in a case like this of Arizona the only way to secure popular rights is through unconditional recognition of States' rights. As regards every question involving National sovereignty under the Constitution, the Federal Government is supreme; but in purely State affairs the State is supreme, and the people of the State should have the absolute right to determine just how they wish their judicial system conducted. It is the negation of popular government to deny the people the right to establish for themselves what their judicial system shall be. Arizona has the absolute right to try the recall, just as any of the existing States has the absolute right to try it or not to try it, and to have an elective or appointive judiciary, as it pleases. To keep Arizona from Statehood because she has adopted the recall as applied to the judiciary is a grave injustice to Arizona, and an assault upon the principles which underlie our whole system of free popular government.

SELECTED BIBLIOGRAPHY

Cross, John L., et al., *Arizona, Its People and Its Resources* (Tucson, 1964)

Lamar, Howard R., *The Far Southwest, 1846-1912: A Territorial History* (New Haven, 1966)

Mann, Dean E., *The Politics of Water in Arizona* (Tucson, 1963)

Martin, Douglas, *An Arizona Chronology: Territorial Years, 1846-1912* (Tucson, 1963)

----- *An Arizona Chronology: Statehood, 1913-1936* (Tucson, 1966)

Miller, Joseph, *Arizona Cavalcade: The Turbulent Times* (New York, 1962)

Poston, Charles D. (John M. Meyers, ed.), *Building a State in Apache Land* (Tempe, Arizona, 1963)

Shadegg, Stephen C., *Arizona: An Adventure in Irrigation* (Phoenix, 1949)

Van Petten, Donald R., *The Constitution and Government of Arizona* (Phoenix, Third ed., 1960)

Wagoner, Jay J., *Arizona Territory, 1846-1912: A Political History* (Tucson, 1970)

NAME INDEX

Ashley, James H., 7
Ashurst, Henry F., 19,30

Bascom, George H., 6
Basconales, Jose de, 1
Bashford, Coles, 8
Baylor, John R., 6
Bean, Curtis C., 12
Bliss, Tasker H., 21
Brodie, Alexander O., 16
Buchanan, James, 5
Burns, M. G., 19

Cameron, Ralph H., 18,25,26
Campbell, John G., 11
Campbell, Thomas E., 22-24
Cardenas, Garcia Lopez de, 1
Carranza, Venustiano, 20
Carson, Kit, 7
Clark, Edward S., 26
Cleveland, Grover, 14,15
Cochise, 6,9
Cook, Nathan B., 4
Cooke, Philip St. George, 3
Coolidge, Calvin, 28
Coronado, Francisco de, 1
Crabb, Henry A., 5
Croix, Teodoro de, 2
Crook, George, 9,13

Douglas, Lewis F., 26,29

Espejo, Antonio de, 1

Fannin, Paul J., 32
Foraker, Joseph, 17
Franklin, Benjamin J., 15

Fremont, John C., 10
Frohmiller, A., 31

Gadsden, James, 4
Garces, Francisco T., 2
Garvey, Dan E., 31
Gatewood, Charles B., 13
Geronimo, 18
Goddard, Samuel P., 32
Goldwater, Barry M., 32
Goodwin, John N., 7,8
Greenway, Isalolla, 28,29
Gurley, John A., 7

Harrison, Benjamin, 13,14
Hayden, Carl, 19,26
Hayes, Rutherford B., 11
Hoover, Herbert, 25,27
House, L., 32
Hoyt, John P., 10
Hughes, Louis C., 14,15
Hunt, George P., 19-22,25-27
Hunter, Sherod, 6

Ickes, Harold L., 29
Irwin, John N., 11,13

Johnson, Lyndon B., 32

Kearny, Stephen W., 3
Kennedy, John F., 32
Kibbey, Joseph M., 17
Kino, Eusebio, 1,2

Lane, Franklin K., 22
Lincoln, Abraham, 6,7
Lowden, Frank O., 24

121

Martin, Cloyd H., 26
McCord, Myron H., 15
McCormick, Robert C., 8,10
McFarland, Ernest W., 30,32
McKinley, William, 15
McWillie, Marcus H., 6
Matthews, W. R., 31
Miles, Nelson A., 13
Mitchell, John N., 33
Moeur, Benjamin B., 28,29
Mowry, Sylvester, 5
Murdock, John R., 30
Murphy, Nathan O., 14-16

Niza, Marcos de, 1

Obregon, General, 21
Onate, Juan de, 1
Osborn, Sidney P., 30,31
Oury, Granville H., 6,12

Pancoast, Charles E., 3
Phillips, John C., 27
Poston, Charles D., 7,8
Pyle, Howard, 31

Reavis, James A., 12
Rivers, Matthew, 23
Roosevelt, F. D., 30
Roosevelt, Th., 16,17

Safford, Anson P. K., 9
Sage, W. H., 21
Sitgreaves, Lorenzo, 4
Sloan, Richard E., 18
Smith, Marcus A., 13,15-17 19,25
Stanford, R. C., 22
Stephens, Hiram S., 10

Taft, William H., 18,19
Tovar, Pedro de, 1
Tritle, Frederick A., 12
Truman, Harry S., 31

Villa, Pancho, 20,21

Williams, J. R., 32,33
Wilson, John F., 15,17
Wilson, Woodrow, 20
Winsor, Mulford, 24
Wolfley, Lewis, 13

Zulick, C. Meyer, 12